I0505322

Bitcoin Cash

"Sound Money to the World"

A book for everyone

By Victor Morgante

First Edition

First published in 2020 by Viev Pty Ltd
© Viev Pty Ltd 2020

The moral rights of the author have been asserted.

All rights reserved. Except as permitted under the Australian Copyright Act 1968 (for example, a fair dealing for the purposes of study, research, criticism or review), no part of this book may be reproduced, stored in a retrieval system, communicated or transmitted in any form or by any means without prior written permission. All inquiries should be made to the author.

Disclaimer

The material in this publication is of the nature of general comment only, and does not represent professional advice. It is not intended to provide specific guidance for particular circumstances and it should not be relied on as the basis for any decision to take action or not take action on any matter that it covers. Readers should obtain professional advice, where appropriate, before making any such decision that may affect them personally or company they represent. To the maximum extent permitted by law, the author and publisher disclaim all responsibility and liability to any person, business or company, arising directly or indirectly from any person taking or not taking action based on the information within, or as omitted by this publication.

ISBN 9798605970125 (Paperback)

Table of Contents

About this book

This book is for anyone who wants to understand Bitcoin and Bitcoin Cash in particular. You are either taking your first steps into the world of cryptocurrencies or you want to know more. If you are like the author, you are highly sceptical of new technologies, and you want the skinny on just about everything before you take a step in any one direction.

This book aims to be educational and offers a commentary on the reporting of key stories as they relate to bitcoin.

A book must have a raison d'être, and this book exists because history is being written at a rapid pace in the cryptocurrency sphere, and Bitcoin Cash is at the forefront of the battle lines of the currency wars that are being waged all around us, even if we are not aware of them.

If you are new to cryptocurrencies, there are unfortunately quite a few things to learn and be aware of, and so this book should help you get up and going with as little fuss as possible. At the same time, this book should make you aware of the risks of effectively being your own bank if you choose to hold cryptocurrency.

I decided to write this book after watching countless videos, visiting many useful websites, and having read article after article about cryptocurrencies. My research was initially for my own edification, and having woken up one day realising that I know more about cryptocurrency than most people on earth, I am writing this book. That is not hard to do in 2020, as most people on Earth are still unaware when it comes to cryptocurrencies. Mostly I have been intrigued by the politics of cryptocurrencies, and I think that the politics alone is worthy of a book. So you will find a decent share of storytelling in here as well.

This book is a compound narrative, and in some cases, highly subjective. Hopefully this book brings forth a narrative that is compelling to those who cannot stand marketing hype, internet trolls and die-hard geek-speak, but rather are looking for a semblance of sanity and stability in the cryptocurrency sphere, where people can choose to use a cryptocurrency in their day to day life, or not, and simply get on with business.

Books have been written about investing in cryptocurrencies. This is not one of those books. Indeed, if you do a search on YouTube for 'Bitcoin Cash' rather than 'Bitcoin', you will find videos about Bitcoin Cash which are not about investing or getting rich, but rather about practically bringing useful money to the world.

Search the web for videos simply on 'Bitcoin' however and you will be bombarded by videos speculating as to how to get rich. I feel that the Bitcoin Cash narrative is different, and is about simply transacting with a currency that the originators hope will be widely used around the world. Some will get rich from that enterprise, but most people will be approaching cryptocurrency from a perspective which reads, *"Is this really for me? How useful is it? Can I use it in my day-to-day life? Why would I use it?"*

The name of this book is "Bitcoin Cash – 'Sound Money to the World', A book for everyone" and it does its best to be about those three things. *Everyone*, because the narrative of cryptocurrencies is a story that actually does affect just about everyone. It is a narrative of how money is created and dispensed, and where cryptocurrencies had their birth in a dream to develop a platform where money does not get devalued to the detriment of the average person holding it, but rather holds its value over time.

Will Bitcoin Cash achieve its goals? We are soon to find out, and I invite you to read on.

Getting started – Download your Wallet

Getting started with Bitcoin Cash is easy. Simply download and install a suitable electronic wallet application onto your smartphone or personal computer and you are up and away. It is free to download most wallets.

You can download a wallet from the internet at https://www.bitcoincash.org/wallets.html . There are dozens of Bitcoin Cash wallets available for download, with the list maintained by www.bitcoincash.org the de facto rallying site for Bitcoin Cash.

The story around Bitcoin Cash gets interesting from the start. I chose to download and install the wallet from Bitcoin.com for my Android phone (https://wallet.bitcoin.com), figuring that Bitcoin.com is a logical place to go to get a wallet if I am interested in Bitcoin. If you are new to cryptocurrencies, then www.bitcoin.com is one of the first places you may go to too, so it is worth talking about the intrigue that site holds from the start.

I was very wary of downloading and installing the Bitcoin.com wallet on my phone, because many people have left negative reviews for the Bitcoin.com wallet app on the Google Play app store, crying *"scam"*. So I researched extensively; including following up on reviews that said that Roger Ver, the Chairman and former CEO of www.bitcoin.com (which affiliated company makes the wallet) was a convicted criminal!

My research shows that much is actually true. Research also shows that Roger Ver is an entrepreneur who is known as *The Bitcoin Jesus* for his extensive evangelising of Bitcoin and the first person in the world to commercially invest in cryptocurrency companies. Being now the owner of a company that employs over 100 people and which company is dedicated to the spread of Bitcoin Cash it seems highly unlikely that Mr Ver would release any sort of 'scam' application which would jeopardise his own company. Stranger things have happened. So choose wisely.

What a way to get started! As you read on you will see that the world of bitcoin is littered with interesting characters with back-stories to match, where confrontation with the law and status quo has been quite common. Whether this proves to be the long term relationship of a technology that some are calling a *revolution*, is yet to be seen, but if that revolution is to be successful then the average person will hold a cryptocurrency wallet. For the average person the story of engaging with bitcoin starts here…downloading your first wallet.

Take away - Roger Ver was convicted in 2002 for selling pest control fire crackers ('explosives') on eBay without a licence and sentenced to 10 months in a federal prison in the USA. Mr Ver's subsequently renounced his U.S. citizenship and left the country.

The confusion of Bitcoin is immediate - there are two primary variants

The Bitcoin.com wallet supports two cryptocurrencies, Bitcoin Cash and Bitcoin Core, and it is confusion over which currency *is* Bitcoin which further drove my research and ultimately this book.

There is an unfolding story within the cryptocurrency arena which seems set to be divisive for some time, and which story contains a mixed and confusing marketing message. The basis for Bitcoin Cash is that its developers are driven to provide fast, cheap and reliable transactions. Bitcoin Core, a competing cryptocurrency, has a narrative which seems, to my mind, to be that of a confused polyglot. This book will save you months of research to understand the difference between the two primary Bitcoin variants. There are at least four main Bitcoin variants, and tens more cryptocurrencies stem from the original Bitcoin.

Take away - You need to make a careful and calculated choice on which wallet you choose for any cryptocurrency, because ultimately you are putting your faith 100% in the company and/or individuals that produce the wallet; that they will not steal your private cryptocurrency information stored with your wallet and all of your currency. See the chapter, 'More on Wallets', for more information.

Take away – Empirical evidence suggests that the risk of a rouge wallet stealing someone's cryptocurrency is real. While writing this book the Apple company removed a wallet for the competing EOS cryptocurrency from its App Store, presumably because of mounting complaints by users that the wallet has stolen their EOS [1].

Be careful with your cryptocurrency wallet and the private information it stores, because with cryptocurrencies, you effectively hold the keys to your own bank. Lose the keys to that virtual bank, and you will have lost your money.

Being your own bank

The question to ask yourself when using a cryptocurrency wallet is whether you trust yourself more than you trust your bank? In some countries the answer might be "Um…yes!" or "What bank?" Either way, it is your responsibility to be responsible with your money and assets.

Take away – Whatever you do, do not delete your wallet application without first having 'backed up' your *private key*, otherwise you will lose all of your Bitcoin Cash and will not be able to retrieve it. The chapter, 'More on Wallets', provides more information on how to back up your private key. As we progress I

---

[1] "Apple quietly removes shady cryptocurrency wallet accused of stealing users' EOS", The Next Web, https://thenextweb.com/hardfork/2018/10/05/apple-cryptocurrency-eos-app-wallet/ , Accessed at 18th October 2018

will explain what private keys are.

Free Bitcoin Cash

You can get some free Bitcoin Cash from https://free.bitcoin.com (about 11 cents US). The process is straight forward and going through the process of doing a cryptocurrency transaction gives you experience in how to manage your cryptocurrency wallet and funds within that wallet.

Take away – Ultimately the value of Bitcoin Cash shown within your wallet is not stored on your device with the app, but rather on an external electronic database, much like with all modern banks. But your private key, effectively a password of sorts to that external ledger, are stored with your application. Lose that private key and you lose your money. Wallets provide a means to make a backup of that private key.

Where can I spend my Bitcoin Cash

Anyone with a Bitcoin Cash wallet can accept payment in Bitcoin Cash. For a curated list of merchants that accept Bitcoin Cash, download the Marco Coino app for your Android or iPhone phone. Download links can be found at https://map.bitcoin.com/

Marco Coino plots on a map places that accept Bitcoin Cash. At the time of wring Marco Coino has over 1000 listings, including coffee shops and bars.

The Accept Bitcoin Cash initiative features hundreds more places that accept Bitcoin Cash. Track to https://acceptbitcoin.cash/

How can I accept Bitcoin Cash as a Merchant?

If you are a merchant you probably do not want to give each of your staff their own wallet, but rather have a centralised merchant solution. Bitcoin.com has a list of solutions for merchants at https://www.bitcoin.com/merchant-solutions/

Bitcoin Cash Meetups

A good way to find a place where you can spend your Bitcoin Cash, and to meet other people who are interested in the currency, find a Bitcoin Cash 'Meetup' group near you. Www.bitcoincash.org is actively involved in assisting to get meetup groups around the world established, and you can search for a group on www.meetup.com

As part of my research in writing this book I attended a meetup in Australia and had a wonderful time. Despite many naysayers around the world saying that you cannot buy a coffee with Bitcoin, there are most definitely coffee shops that accept Bitcoin Cash, and the meetup I attended was at one such café.

I found the group of people that I met very interesting. A mixture of business people, libertarians and entrepreneurs, the conversation was lively. We bought drinks and food with Bitcoin Cash and discussed the currency, the economics and politics of money.

The biggest take away for me at the meetup was that those in attendance were all in agreement that of all the cryptocurrencies on earth most likely to succeed in meeting the demands of everyday people, Bitcoin Cash was that cryptocurrency. Here we were doing everyday things like drinking, eating and being merry with cryptocurrency as the medium of payment.

Their belief in Bitcoin Cash is to be believed if taken from the view that Bitcoin Cash meetups are well orchestrated around the world that a small economy revolves around the existence of the meetups themselves.

Who owns Bitcoin?

By now you are probably asking, *"What is bitcoin?"* and *"Who owns Bitcoin? Does any one person or company own Bitcoin Cash?"*

No. Nobody owns Bitcoin Cash. Nobody and no company own 'Bitcoin' as a trademark. No one company or person controls Bitcoin Cash, but influential players will affect the success or failure of Bitcoin Cash, and so it pays to know who those players are. We explore those players and their influence over Bitcoin Cash in this book.

Effectively, Bitcoin Cash exists as an electronic network, and you tap into that network to hold and exchange value/currency on what is known as a *decentralised and distributed database.* Because that database stores transactions of value exchange, much as with a bank, the ledger is known as a public distributed ledger. Because no government or bank authorised by a government owns the Bitcoin Cash network, Bitcoin Cash is sometimes known as a *People's Bank.*

It is also natural to ask *"Why was there a split between Bitcoin Cash and Bitcoin Core?"* We cover that as the story rolls on, but first let us look closer at bitcoin and cryptocurrencies.

A People's Bank?

It is common within the bitcoin sphere to read of a *bitcoin community* as if all semblance of formality has been stripped away from the process of banking and managing money. There are many reasons why this nomenclature has arisen, and predominantly it stems back to the beginning of bitcoin itself. We cover that beginning in the next chapter. Here, we assert that because bitcoin is currently open to anyone to participate in the network, and because formal government or government legislated organisations do not run the bitcoin network, it may be useful to think of bitcoin as a *people's bank* with users of that bank forming the *community*.

But, as we will see, the cost of running the bitcoin computer network is actually becoming an expensive exercise and out of reach of the common person. Now attracting large corporations dedicated to running the network and for profit, the notion of a *people's bank* is largely blurred. Only 11 years old, bitcoin has also yet to feel the force of regulation in many jurisdictions, which will ultimately blur the line between what belongs to the people and what the government has influence over.

For those that are asking at this stage, let us now address, *"What is Bitcoin?"*

What is Bitcoin?

Bitcoin is a peer-to-peer electronic cash regime that allows you to transfer value/money to other people, ostensibly without a trusted third-party intermediary (e.g. a bank). Bitcoin Cash is bitcoin, and is one of over 5000 cryptocurrencies that are in existence as of 2020, and there are four main strands of Bitcoin; Bitcoin Cash, Bitcoin Core, Bitcoin Gold, and Bitcoin Diamond.

Bitcoin works *ostensibly* without a trusted third-party intermediary, because ultimately you *do* trust in the people who wrote the software in which you are entrusting the value of your money. As you read on, it will become clear that powerful people make critical decisions over the future of cryptocurrencies and that trust has not been transferred from banks to software or the common man; but rather you must back the right team developing the software of a cryptocurrency if you want to use that cryptocurrency.

Bitcoin is both the name of the cryptocurrency and the computer network (the hardware and software) that runs the cryptocurrency. This is true for all the variants of bitcoin, including Bitcoin Cash. So Bitcoin Cash is the name of a currency and the computer network that runs the currency.

Anyone with a suitable computer and access to the internet can run Bitcoin Cash software and it is the collective whole of all the computers around the world running the bitcoin software network that is also known as the Bitcoin Cash network. Each computer running the software is a *peer* in a peer-to-peer network.

In this book we are going to be talking predominantly about Bitcoin Cash, and wherever you read Bitcoin, you can read Bitcoin Cash. That much in itself is controversial, and as you read on you will see that Bitcoin Cash makes the suitable claim to being Bitcoin.

Take away - Where you read the words 'currency' and 'money' in this book, you should also be aware that in countries like Australia, those methods of asset exchange that involve what people call a 'cryptocurrency' are not considered legal tender by the government, but rather bitcoin is classed as an *asset* that can be bought, sold and transferred; and which may incur a capital gain or loss when it comes to tax purposes. To be clear, in countries like Australia, a cryptocurrency is not considered money or currency by the government, even though you may use it as a means of value exchange [2]. For our purposes we will speak of cryptocurrencies as currencies in this book.

What is a cryptocurrency?

A cryptocurrency is merely a currency that is exchanged over a computer network and which uses some form of cryptography to help secure transactions over that network. The name is a bit of a misnomer, because all fiscal electronic transaction networks use some form of cryptography in their makeup, and most currencies on Earth have an electronic format. For now, suffice yourself that cryptocurrencies distinguish themselves by not relying on traditional networks as provided by companies such as Visa or MasterCard, as authorised by any government or as provided by any bank.

We cover the details of how a cryptocurrency like Bitcoin works as you read on, but if you merely wish to be satisfied that a cryptocurrency is some form of useful electronic currency, then the take away is that the Bitcoin network has been successfully used for the exchange of value between people for 11 years.

Bitcoin is the first successful peer-to-peer electronic cash system subsequently called a cryptocurrency.

---

[2] https://www.ato.gov.au/General/Gen/Tax-treatment-of-crypto-currencies-in-Australia---specifically-bitcoin/?anchor=Transactingwithcryptocurrency#Transactingwithcryptocurrency , Australian Taxation Office, Accessed at 18th October 2018

Security of the network

While it would be good to say that the Bitcoin network has had 11 years of failsafe electronic cash transactions, this is not exactly true. Part of the reason Bitcoin Cash split from Bitcoin Core is inherent security concerns with merchants accepting Bitcoin Core payments. There are means, however, under which both Bitcoin Core and Bitcoin Cash are inherently safe to handle transactions and we cover that further in this work.

Take away - Under some circumstances the Bitcoin Core network can be compromised for payments received by merchants. Customers can effectively walk out the door with goods 'purchased' using Bitcoin Core, and then return the money to themselves. Bitcoin Cash is far less likely to be compromised at the merchant transaction level. See the video at https://www.youtube.com/watch?v=lLkiu8zs318 for more information. In January 2020 the reporter Graham Smith wrote an article for news.bitcoin.com which admits that under certain circumstances it is possible to compromise the Bitcoin Cash network also [3]. So as with fraudulent 'charge backs' within the Visa and MasterCard payment networks, there are risks with bitcoin that warrant attention.

Keep reading this chapter and the next to learn how best to protect yourself again what are known as 'double spend' attacks on the Bitcoin Cash network.

In essence, the longer a transaction exists on the distributed public ledger of bitcoin the more secure a payment.

---

[3] Smith, Graham, "Why double spending on BCH and BTC aren't the same", news.bitcoin.com, https://news.bitcoin.com/why-double-spending-on-bch-and-btc-arent-the-same-problem/, Accessed at 17th January 2020

Why are there four main Bitcoin networks?

What a mess. Up until a few years ago, there was only one Bitcoin, but because the Bitcoin software is 'open source' (so that anyone can verify and copy the software), people decided to create their own versions of Bitcoin to suit their own needs, including philosophical and economic outlook, political persuasion, ego and greed. Of course, some of those Bitcoin copies kept the name 'Bitcoin' in their name. Many of the more than 5000 cryptocurrencies in existence use the Bitcoin source software code as the basis for the software that runs those networks. In this book, we are not interested in any bitcoin variant other than Bitcoin Cash and the reasons for that will become apparent as you read on. For now, you should be at least aware that the heritage of Bitcoin Cash traces back to the very beginning of Bitcoin and that those people who effectively control the destiny of Bitcoin Cash hold dear to the principal that Bitcoin Cash is 'Sound Money for the World'. We examine whether that is true or not as we explore Bitcoin Cash more deeply.

While perhaps confusing that there is more than one Bitcoin, if seen through a lens where *dollar* is a name shared by more than one traditional currency, the atmosphere becomes less confusing. For instance, there is the Australian dollar, the U.S. dollar, and the Canadian dollar. In the same way, there is more than one Bitcoin.

Your job, should you choose to use Bitcoin, is to decide which Bitcoin you wish to use.

Take away – If you are starting out with cryptocurrencies you are faced with quite a serious question, *"Which cryptocurrency should I choose to use?"* If you settle on one of the Bitcoin variants, be aware that a predominant distinction to clarify is which currency has the most utility. Bitcoin Cash is touted as costing less per transaction as Bitcoin Core and developed for widespread commerce, while holding onto the notion that it is an effective *store of value*. I.e. The value stored in Bitcoin Cash should hold its value over time. Empirical evidence suggests that

Bitcoin Cash is indeed very cheap to transact with, costing less than 1 cent US per transaction, and where next to no cryptocurrency on Earth has been an effective store of value throughout the year 2018, but have been in other years. That is, the relative value of cryptocurrencies is currently quite volatile but some cryptocurrencies have been very effective stores of value over time. We will cover both of those concepts as we move through the book.

Let us explore deeper as to what is Bitcoin Cash and cryptocurrencies in general.

What is Bitcoin Cash?

If you live in a Western country or any country with electricity, banking and a telecommunications network, then you are to some extent already familiar with electronic or digital currency. If you do your banking online, then you are very familiar with electronic currency. If you use a credit or debit card at an EFTPOS (Electronic Funds Transfer Point of Sale) machine, then you are already familiar with electronic/digital currency. Bitcoin Cash is just another way of storing and transferring value between people electronically. The fact that cryptocurrencies have 'crypto' (short for 'cryptographic') in their name should not confuse you, because all sophisticated electronic funds/value transfer systems use some form of cryptography in their makeup. There is nothing especially remarkable about Bitcoin Cash in that regard, other than that it is especially inexpensive to transact with as long as you stay within the currency. Like any currency however, as you exchange that currency for any other currency, there is generally a cost associated with that exchange.

There is a vast array of cryptocurrency exchanges around the world for which you can exchange central bank/government issued currencies (such as the Australian dollar) for cryptocurrencies. Costs of exchange range anywhere from 0.1% to 5% [4], and in that respect transacting with a cryptocurrency may be no less expensive as when transacting with typical technologies if you exchange currency for each transaction you make. Such costs, if you adopt that strategy, bring transacting with a cryptocurrency in line with transacting with Visa and MasterCard; however if you make repeated transactions within Bitcoin Cash, and do not exchange between currencies, your costs will be very low indeed when compared to other electronic currency transaction tools.

---

[4] https://www.finder.com.au/cryptocurrency/exchanges

What distinguishes Bitcoin Cash, and other similar cryptocurrencies, is that Bitcoin Cash does not rely on any one trusted third-party intermediary in order to effect the transfer of funds/value between people. If you have a Bitcoin Cash wallet on your phone, and so does your friend, you can send Bitcoin Cash to them directly. In that respect, Bitcoin Cash can be considered as good as traditional cash.

Of course, because anyone with a smartphone can download a cryptocurrency wallet and begin transferring value with other people, without having first had to show three forms of identification as is typically required when setting up a bank account, governments, police, security services and regulators around the world are very concerned about cryptocurrencies and their use. This is because of concerns over money laundering and funding of criminal activity. Cash economies have always attracted such attention and will continue to do so. But there is a problem for governments…

The problem for governments, or *benefit to the people* as some may see it, is that there is effectively no way of stopping people from using cryptocurrencies. Anyone can send any amount of Bitcoin Cash to anyone else in the world with a Bitcoin Cash wallet, and it is next to impossible for anyone to stop that happening. Cryptocurrencies exist, are functional and it seems that they are never going away. The *genie is out of the bottle* so to speak. Because anyone in the world with a computer/smartphone and access to the internet can use a cryptocurrency, it seems that cryptocurrencies are really here to stay, and we will explore why. In the mean time, governments form regulations and it is up to citizens to abide by those regulations.

Bitcoin Cash is just one cryptocurrency and has one of the largest market capitalisations in the world. At the time of writing the value of the Bitcoin Cash market is over U.S. $8 billion with over 17 million Bitcoin Cash in circulation [5].

---

[5] See https://coinmarketcap.com/ for the Bitcoin Cash market capitalisation.

Take away – Track to https://www.bitcoincash.org/ and www.association.cash for more information on Bitcoin Cash.

What is peculiar to Bitcoin Cash and similar cryptocurrencies is that Bitcoin Cash is pseudo-anonymous, and, like cash, transactions in Bitcoin Cash can be achieved with a certain degree of privacy. This parallel to cash transactions was one of the initial reasons for the development of bitcoin. Before we look at that development, let us consider whether cryptocurrencies are here to stay.

Cryptocurrencies are here to Stay

If you are new to cryptocurrencies, the biggest questions that you are probably asking yourself are, *"Can I trust cryptocurrencies?"*, *"Do I waste my time learning about cryptocurrencies?"* and *"Is this just geek money that will likely disappear in the near future?"*

These are all valid questions and any reasonable person would and should ask them.

After having done extensive research for my own benefit in writing this book, I can safely say that cryptocurrencies are not going away. Some may fade away because of lack of interest and use, but cryptocurrencies, in general, are well and truly entrenched into the mindset of enough people, and generating such considerable revenues for some commercial players, that they are not going away. Cryptocurrencies are here to stay. Let us look at why.

Some governments have banned cryptocurrencies[6], but many Western countries have accepted their existence by opening ways

---

[6] Randal, Lila, "Bitcoin Latest: Saudi Arabia bans cryptocurrency in major crackdown - warning issued", The Express, https://www.express.co.uk/news/world/1002951/bitcoin-news-saudi-arabia-

for commerce to flourish using cryptocurrencies, with the supposed expectation that embracing technological innovation will open doors for future commerce and ultimately tax revenue. Of course, there is likely the understanding by governments of the world that a *cash society* will flourish like it or not; and so it is better to regulate an industry and try and contain it somehow than deny its existence altogether.

You can get a feel for how radically cryptocurrencies are changing the world by verifying for yourself that nearly all sophisticated governments of the world now either have regulations that govern their use or are in the process of drafting those regulations. For a state of play for many countries, simply go to the following Wikipedia page and check for the status of regulation over cryptocurrencies in your country:

https://en.wikipedia.org/wiki/Legality_of_bitcoin_by_country_or_territory

Take away – Three videos on YouTube should convince you that governments of the world are taking cryptocurrencies seriously. Each covers a senate hearing committee focused on Bitcoin and cryptocurrencies for the countries of the United States of America, Canada and Australia:

1. U.S.A.: https://www.youtube.com/watch?v=VcLycY0hIGc
2. Canada: https://www.youtube.com/watch?v=xUNGFZDO8mM&t=24s
3. Australia: https://www.youtube.com/watch?v=6rGHSpC5uNk

Take away – For up-to-date news reports on the impact of cryptocurrencies throughout the world, I find the news service at bitcoin.com (https://news.bitcoin.com) very informative.

---

cryptocurrency-ban , Accessed at 18th October 2018

Overall, what lends me to believe that cryptocurrencies are here to stay are the following:

1. Geeks having the allure of creating their own currency;

   It takes considerable technical know-how to create and maintain a cryptocurrency. From what I can tell, there is a suitably large group of people who are enthralled by the technical challenge of cryptocurrencies and motivated to create them. Find a suitably technical person, mix in a touch of entrepreneurship, and you have one more cryptocurrency. As noted, there are over 5000 cryptocurrencies in the world as at 2020 [7]. I cannot see this ever going away. The allure of perhaps becoming famous, rich or both is just too strong for some to resist. Individual cryptocurrencies will come and go, but the market category is here to stay.

2. Libertarians reaching for any mechanism which will reduce the power of governments to exercise control over them;

   When I first started researching cryptocurrencies, I did not know what a *libertarian* was, although intuitively you can get a picture of who a libertarian is by the name:

   "Libertarianism (from Latin: libertas, meaning "freedom") is a collection of political philosophies and movements that uphold liberty as a core principle. Libertarians seek to maximize political freedom and autonomy" [8]

   The genesis of Bitcoin has its roots in someone seeming to have been extremely dissatisfied with the status quo of government and central bank issued currencies, which we will

---

[7] The site, www.coinmarketcap.com maintains a count of the currently known cryptocurrencies in circulation, https://coinmarketcap.com, Accessed at 17th January 2020.

[8] Libertarianism, Wikipedia, https://en.wikipedia.org/wiki/Libertarianism#cite_note-1, Accessed at 18th October 2018

delve into later. Whether a libertarian or not, the initial creator of bitcoin manifest a new type of money that is very attractive to libertarians. One where it is practically impossible to stop transactions between holders of bitcoin wallets. I cannot see this ever going away. There will always be libertarians, and they will always choose to usurp government control with their own way of doing business where they can.

3. The vast amount of money spent on the technical (computer) infrastructure that supports cryptocurrencies:

   As at 2020, billions of dollars has been spent by individuals and companies on computer equipment that supports cryptocurrencies such as Bitcoin Cash. This alone would not ensure that cryptocurrencies are here to stay, but as you will realise as you read on, the people operating that equipment are highly incentivised to promote the cryptocurrency networks they operate over, and keep them running.

   While a commercial imperative exists, and if they remain legal and profitable, cryptocurrencies will exist on Earth.

   Take away – While Bitcoin Cash has a market capitalisation of over U.S. $8 billion, at the time of writing, the cryptocurrency market as a whole has a capitalisation of over U.S. $100 billion. You can see the market capitalisation of a vast number of exchange traded cryptocurrencies at https://coinmarketcap.com. You can see up to date exchange rates for many cryptocurrencies at www.tradingview.com

   Take away –While bitcoin is 11 years old at time of writing, and that may not seem to be a long time, in 2 years time there will not be a teenager alive who has never lived in a world without bitcoin, in the same way that no teenager alive today has lived in a world without the internet.

How did Cryptocurrencies arrive?

A cryptocurrency is merely a means of electronically exchanging value, commensurate, one way or another, with money or currency, and which uses some sort of cryptography in its makeup. If fact bitcoin does not encrypt information to hide anything, but rather uses a branch of mathematics stemming from cryptographic research which allows for *digital signatures*. Within its distributed ledger, bitcoin is allocated to signatures much the same way as money is allocated to numbers in a Swiss bank account. Rather than hide anything cryptographically, it is more accurate to say that you only know who owns bitcoin if you know who has access to the signatures the bitcoin is allocated against. So, again, cryptocurrency is a bit of a misnomer.

The first widely accepted cryptocurrency, Bitcoin (or written as lowercase, bitcoin, to fit with convention for currencies), was released to the world on 3th January 2009, by its inventor, Satoshi Nakamoto. The name Satoshi Nakamoto is most likely pseudonymous, and the impact of Nakamoto's invention is such that it has already changed world history.

There was, in 2009, nothing new whatsoever about the electronic exchange of currency and using some form of cryptography. Every time you log into your bank account on a web browser and see the prefix of the domain name you logged into as https://, you are using a form of cryptography to secure the information shared between you and the bank's web server. Cryptography is used to secure the network infrastructure that banks use to process billions of dollars worth of transactions around the world each day.

What set bitcoin apart was that it was the first time that anyone had successfully configured an arrangement of technologies and procedures in such a way that no central authority or intermediary, such as bank, was needed in order to transact value safely over the network. Bitcoin does not rely on a trusted government, bank or company to provide the network over which to transact, it merely relies on computers connected to the internet. With the arrival of bitcoin, you can exchange value between personal computers connected to the internet in such a way that the transactions have high validity. The transactions, in general, are trusted by each member using the network. *In general*, because by design, once the bitcoin network got to a certain size and distribution it became practically impossible for a malicious party to defraud the network or for a government to shut down. *In general*, because, as we have covered, ways to defraud users of the bitcoin networks have been uncovered. *In general*, because there are ways to protect yourself against being defrauded.

NB Some bitcoin networks, such as Bitcoin Gold, did not reach a critical network size in their development and have been defrauded to the tune of millions of dollars [9]. More on that further in this book. Firstly, let us take a step back to the beginning of bitcoin.

But how did a virtual people's bank arrive out of seemingly nowhere? Where did bitcoin come from? How did it start?

Bitcoin – A peer-to-peer electronic cash system

The machinations of the bitcoin network were outlined in an academically stylised white paper called, *"Bitcoin – A peer-to-peer electronic cash system"*, written by a person or persons going by the name of Satoshi Nakamoto. In October 2008 Nakamoto released the paper to a cryptography mailing list.

We pause the story here. This is interesting. What is a mailing list? What mailing list? Why was it important to release the paper

---

[9] Redman, Jamie, Bittrex to delist Bitcoin Gold over 51% attack, News.bitcoin.com, https://news.bitcoin.com/bittrex-to-delist-bitcoin-gold-over-51-attack/, Accessed at 18th October 2018

to that mailing list? Who is Satoshi Nakamoto? What is a white paper?

An electronic mailing list is generally a list of email addresses to which people send emails, but facilities exist on the internet which allow people to subscribe to a mailing list such that more than one person can distribute emails to other people on the mailing list. Such mailing lists act as an online forum where ideas can be shared between people via email. Generally people subscribe to a mailing list that focuses discussions on a particular area of interest. Nakamoto shared the bitcoin paper on a mailing list focusing on cryptography. At the time of releasing the paper, Nakamoto had not released the bitcoin software; that came second.

From my research, the best information I can find is that Nakamoto shared the white paper on a mailing list hosted at the domain name, metzdowd.com [10] [11], which at the time of writing is a domain that hosts no html pages. It seems that metzdowd.com still hosts a mailing list however. A veil of privacy seems to surround the domain itself. This dichotomy goes some way to shedding light on the privacy concerns common to the type of people who used such a mailing list, cryptographers and *cypherpunks*.

Nakamoto's original post can be seen at: http://www.metzdowd.com/pipermail/cryptography/2008-October/014810.html. If you cannot access that, luckily for historians the mailing list was connected to an online archiving service, such that we can see the original email at https://www.mail-archive.com/cryptography@metzdowd.com/msg09959.html.

Nakamoto's email begins:

"I've been working on a new electronic cash system that's fully

---

[10] https://en.bitcoin.it/wiki/Bitcoin
[11] https://bitcointalk.org/index.php?topic=353311.0

peer-to-peer, with no trusted third party.

The paper is available at:
http://www.bitcoin.org/bitcoin.pdf "

You can still go to the bitcoin.org address and read the white paper. It is 9 pages long if you want to read it.

What is a White Paper?

An academically stylised paper is a document written in such a way that it may be submitted to a journal for anonymous peer review and publication if accepted by persons considered qualified to judge over the quality of the document. The practice of submitting a paper for anonymous peer review stems back over 100 years. Famous authors of papers, for instance, include Albert Einstein who published his first set of famous papers in the Annalen der Physik scientific journal in 1905. Initially printed on paper, of course today journals and their papers are published both in print and as electronic documents.

A *white paper*, on the other hand, is a paper stylised in a similar fashion to a peer reviewed paper, but which is not of a standard that would normally qualify for journal publication and is not submitted to a journal for review and publishing, sometimes intentionally. White papers are a general outline of a proposal and which describe the technicalities of the proposal. Nakamoto's paper is better viewed as a white paper because the paper was never submitted to a journal for publication, although clearly written to be reviewed and accepted by those Nakamoto considered peers. In deciding not to have the paper reviewed for journal publication, Nakamoto was probably simply making a statement which read, *"Here is bitcoin. Here is what I've been working on. Like it or not, here it is".*

So Satoshi Nakamoto shared the paper on a cryptography mailing list, and to this day it remains unclear whom Nakamoto is. It is generally agreed that Satoshi Nakamoto is a pseudonym and of someone who was particularly private, at least early in the bitcoin story, because nobody named Satoshi Nakamoto has ever been found and who would qualify as the person having released the paper or the original bitcoin software.

Nakamoto was reaching out to other people to share the bitcoin idea with, and looking for acceptance of the idea at the same time. So why did Nakamoto choose the cryptography mailing list to seek acceptance of bitcoin?

In retrospect it makes a lot of sense. Bitcoin relies on a branch of cryptography to provide security over the value stored in bitcoin, which are effectively electronic data as record of value stored and accessible to people with the appropriate cryptographic keys to access that data. So Nakamoto was reaching out to people who would understand the bitcoin invention, specialists in cryptography.

But the story is richer than that. Some of the very same people who would be interested in the cryptographic aspects of bitcoin would also subscribe to the viewpoints shared by cypherpunks, who by and large used cryptography in their work.

But what is a cypherpunk?

To the best of anyone's knowledge, the term cypherpunk was coined by a computer hacker and author, Jude Milhon (better known by her pseudonym St. Jude) describing a group of people she had become associated with who were all interested in cryptography. Largely exposed by stories written for Wired Magazine by Steven Levy and Rosie Cross in the 1990s, Cypherpunks materialised as mysterious figures who worked in the shadows and bold things to say about the world around them.

The word *Cypherpunk* is noted as a play on the word cipher/cypher, a term from cryptography, and *cyberpunk* a genre of science fiction. As the name of the genre, cyberpunk is about "lowlife and high-tech", but Lawrence Person describes, in his

"Notes Toward a Postcyberpunk Manifesto", a cyberpunk as (and to paraphrase) *a marginalized, alienated loner living on the edge of society in a dystopic [sic] future where daily life is impacted by rapid technological change, an ubiquitous datasphere [sic] of computerized information, and invasive modification of the human body."* [12]

Cypherpunks most likely do not align themselves as lowlife or body modifiers. The original cypherpunks were seemingly successful people with a common interest in cryptography and privacy. But parallels can be drawn with cyberpunks when it comes to the electrotechnology age.

Cypherpunks have come to represent cryptographers who share a common concern about the power of governments and concern of a dystopian future where governments and companies have unreasonable access and control over data and where cryptography offers the way to maintain privacy over data. Some may argue that dystopian future has already arrived [13]. But it had not in 1992.

The story goes that in late 1992, three individuals, Eric Hughes, Timothy May, and John Gilmore, invited twenty of their friends to an informal meeting to discuss some of what they considered the world's most vexing computer programming and cryptographic issues. Eric Hughes was a mathematician from University of California, May a retired businessman who had worked at Intel, and Gilmore a computer scientist who was Sun Microsystems' fifth employee. Their initial meeting eventually evolved into a monthly meeting held at John Gilmore's company,

---

[12] Person, Lawrence (October 8, 1999). "Notes Toward a Postcyberpunk Manifesto". Slashdot. Originally published in Nova Express, issue 16 (1998), https://slashdot.org/story/99/10/08/2123255/notes-toward-a-postcyberpunk-manifesto , Accessed at 18th October 2018

[13] As an example of an author arguing that we live in a somewhat dystopian society already see Lujan, Sterlin's (18th October 2018), "The value of uncensorable technology in an age of censorship", news.bitcoin.com, https://news.bitcoin.com/the-value-of-uncensorable-technology-in-an-age-of-censorship/, Accessed at 18th October 2018

Cygnus Solutions, and where at one of the first meetings, Jude Milhon coined the term *cypherpunks* to describe the group. [14] [15] [16]

Timothy May eventually published, in 1994, a set of answers to frequently asked questions (FAQs) asked of the group, listing the basic issues that the group was trying to solve and as he saw them.

Within the answers to FAQs, May states that:

"Cryptology is a fairly technical subject, and one can no more jump in and expect to be taken seriously without any preparation than in any other technical field."

He was answering a question as to why existing members of the group were sometimes short with new members of the group, but also setting an expectation that acceptance into the group was difficult and was achieved by merit.

We can safely assume that Nakamoto submitted the bitcoin whitepaper to the cryptography mailing list chosen because Nakamoto was seeking acceptance of his/her/their ideas, and that Nakamoto perhaps shared the views of cypherpunks over issues that cypherpunks were tackling.

As May describes the issues, they were [17]:

"+ [The] Great Divide: privacy vs. compliance with laws

---

[14] Bartlett, Jamie, "Cypherpunks Write Code", American Scientist (March-April 2016), https://www.americanscientist.org/article/cypherpunks-write-code, Accessed at 18th October 2018

[15] Levy, Steven (01/02/1993); "Crypto Rebels"; Wired Magazine; https://www.wired.com/1993/02/crypto-rebels/ , Accessed at Thursday, 18 October 2018

[16] Cross, Rosie. (01/02/1995), "Modem Grrrl", Wired Magazine, https://www.wired.com/1995/02/st-jude/ , Accessed at Thursday, 18 October 2018

[17] May, Timothy, "Cyphernomicon", https://nakamotoinstitute.org/static/docs/cyphernomicon.txt, Accessed at 16th October 2018

+ free speech and privacy, even if means some criminals cannot be caught (a stand the U.S. Constitution was strongly in favor of, at one time)

- a man's home is his castle...the essence of the Magna Carta systems...rights of the individual to be secure from random searches

+ or invasive tactics to catch criminals, regulate behavior, and control the population

- the legitimate needs to enforce laws, to respond to situations

+ this parallels the issue of self-protection vs. protection by law and police - as seen in the gun debate

- crypto = guns in the sense of being an individual's preemptive[sic] protection - past the point of no return

- Strong crypto as building material for a new age

+ Transnationalism and Increased Degrees of Freedom - governments can't hope to control movements and communications of citizens; borders are transparent"

It seems that Nakamoto shared the view that privacy was paramount. In his introductory email Nakamoto says of bitcoin:

```
"Double-spending is prevented with a peer-to-peer
network.
 No mint or other trusted parties [are required
for bitcoin].
 Participants can be anonymous."
```

(bold highlighting added)

"Participants can be anonymous" and *"No mint or other trusted party";* clearly Nakamoto's *new electronic cash* system was designed with privacy in mind. By inventing a currency that runs on the internet without trusted parties, Nakamoto was also ensuring that bitcoin is borderless and transnational. Nakamoto's views on central banks and government issued currency is shared in later emails by Nakamoto, but Nakamoto had found her audience; an audience ready primed to help Nakamoto achieve his aim, an audience dedicated to privacy and writing computer

software using encryption to achieve that aim. What better place to launch bitcoin? What better set of peers to share his views?

What better place indeed. The cypherpunk movement had been in full swing for over 15 years when Nakamoto released his paper. We do not know exactly Nakamoto is, but many assume that Nakamoto was very familiar with the cypherpunk movement before turning up as Satoshi Nakamoto. For anyone knows, Nakamoto may well have been a well known figure within the cypherpunk movement before moving to a pseudonym to announce bitcoin. The cypherpunk movement attracted some of the smartest minds in the cryptography arena, and some of the most well known. Noteworthy amongst them being Julian Assange of WikiLeaks fame. Going by the name of "Proff" Assange frequented the mailing list hosted on toad.com (setup by Hughes) well before setting up WikiLeaks [18]. Assange was known for having co-written an encryption system known as Rubberhose, a type of *deniable encryption* system allowing the holder of the keys to encrypted plain text on a computer hard-drive to plausibly deny the existence of any encrypted text being on the hard-drive at all. In 2013 and 2016, and likely spurred by the rise of bitcoin, authors revisited the cypherpunks with Jamie Bartlett of American Scientist and a cypherpunk sounding *R. U. Sirius* of the Verge writing articles for their respective publications, trudging through the escapades of the cypherpunks [19] [20].

---

[18] Emails from Julian Assange on cypherpunk mailing lists, http://cryptome.org/0001/assange-cpunks.htm, Accessed at Friday, 17 January 2020.
 [19] Sirius,R. U. (07/03/2013), Cypherpunk rising: WikiLeaks, encryption, and the coming surveillance dystopia, The Verge, https://www.theverge.com/2013/3/7/4036040/cypherpunks-julian-assange-wikileaks-encryption-surveillance-dystopia, Accessed at Thursday, 18 October 2018
 [20] Bartlett, Jamie, "Cypherpunks Write Code", American Scientist, March-April 2016, Volume 104, Number 2, Pg 120, https://www.americanscientist.org/article/cypherpunks-write-code, Accessed at Thursday, 18 October 2018

That Nakamoto supported many of the ideals of cypherpunks, especially where it comes to privacy and not trusting institutions such as banks, can be readily gleaned from a post that Nakamoto released on a separate peer-to-peer networking website in a similar timeframe [21]. It reads in part:

"The root problem with conventional currency is all the trust that's required to make it work. The central bank must be trusted not to debase the currency, but the history of fiat currencies is full of breaches of that trust. Banks must be trusted to hold our money and transfer it electronically, but they lend it out in waves of credit bubbles with barely a fraction in reserve. We have to trust them with our privacy, trust them not to let identity thieves drain our accounts. Their massive overhead costs make micropayments impossible.

A generation ago, multi-user time-sharing computer systems had a similar problem. Before strong encryption, users had to rely on password protection to secure their files, placing trust in the system administrator to keep their information private. Privacy could always be overridden by the admin based on his judgment call weighing the principle of privacy against other concerns, or at the behest of his superiors. Then strong encryption became available to the masses, and trust was no longer required. Data could be secured in a way that was physically impossible for others to access, no matter for what reason, no matter how good the excuse, no matter what.

It's time we had the same thing for money. With e-currency based on cryptographic proof, without the need to trust a third party middleman, money can be secure and transactions effortless."

---

[21] Nakamoto's post to the P2P Foundation shortly after releasing the bitcoin software, http://p2pfoundation.ning.com/forum/topics/bitcoin-open-source, Accessed at 18 October 2018

That Nakamoto was well aware of the viewpoint of libertarians can be gleaned from his words in an early email to the mailing list. He says of bitcoin:

```
"It's very attractive to the libertarian viewpoint if
we can explain it properly." 22
```

Quite obviously Nakamoto also shared the cypherpunk view that privacy is king. In response to someone posting on the cryptography mailing list that: *"You will not find a solution to political problems in cryptography"*, Nakamoto simply responded:

```
"Yes, but we can win a major battle in the arms
race and gain a new territory of freedom for
several years.

Governments are good at cutting off the heads of a
centrally controlled networks like Napster, but
pure P2P networks like Gnutella and Tor seem to be
holding their own." 23
```

In fact, conversation about bitcoin and its implications for change became excited on the mailing list the very day after Nakamoto posted her first email. The conversation ranged from sceptical to highly supportive; those in support immediately recognising the value of Nakamoto's vision.

Fortunately for historians, again, the first reactions to Nakamoto's paper can be found at

---

[22] Nakamoto's awareness of a libertarian viewpoint. Mail to the metzdown.com mailing list, http://www.metzdowd.com/pipermail/cryptography/2008-November/014853.html, Accessed at Monday, 22 October 2018
[23] Nakamoto post on the metzdowd cryptography mailing list, https://www.mail-archive.com/cryptography@metzdowd.com/msg09971.html, Accessed at Sunday, 21 October 2018

The very first reaction to Nakamoto's first email is what draws this history of Bitcoin to that of Bitcoin Cash. Bitcoin Cash *is* bitcoin, and became so because of what has subsequently come to be known as *The Great Scaling Debate*. It seems that this was almost inevitable, as the very first email response to Nakamoto's seminal email reads:

```
"We very, very much need such a system, but the way I
understand your proposal, it does not seem to scale to the
required size." 24
```

Nakamoto disagreed with that analysis [25], but what were they talking about? What is *scaling* and why was it important?

Scaling, when it comes to computer software, is the ability for that software (and the network supporting the software) to handle a large throughput of data. In the case of bitcoin, the subsequent debate was over whether or not the design of the bitcoin software and peer-to-peer network could support a large throughput of data. In the case of bitcoin, that data represents transactions, transactions that record whether the holder of bitcoin transfers all or part of that bitcoin to another holder. We come back to the scaling debate in a few chapters, but first let us look closer again at what Nakamoto had achieved.

Nakamoto's white paper

Nakamoto's seminal white paper on bitcoin was never released for anonymous peer review for publication in a journal, but rather

---

[24] Beginning of the Great Scaling Debate, http://www.metzdowd.com/pipermail/cryptography/2008-November/014814.html, Accessed at Sunday, 21 October 2018
[25] Nakamoto on scaling, http://www.metzdowd.com/pipermail/cryptography/2008-November/014815.html

as a publicly available white paper. It seems that the decision to do so was intentional. Papers submitted for review for publication in a journal generally must meet a very high standard for publication. They must at least meet the quality standard of the journal itself. Some journals have a higher reputation than others and where the criteria for acceptance of papers are judiciously policed by those *peers* deemed suitable to review papers for the journal. It was evident from the very start that Nakamoto's white paper did not meet the criteria required for journal publication, even though the paper has subsequently been referred to by many as a work of genius. Why is that?

The day after Nakamoto's paper was released to the mailing list, Nakamoto began to receive comments and questions about the paper. Cryptographers, such as Hal Finney (a well known cryptographer), enthusiastically lent support to the bitcoin proposal, while asking for confirmation on details of the specifics of how things would work under the software. Nakamoto seemed to have solved what top cryptographers had failed to solve, but the paper itself did not have all the detail.

Others were interested but critical, claiming that the paper did not provide enough information to qualify the quality of the proposal. What is interesting is that no time was wasted in getting back to Nakamoto with feedback; the questions and interest were immediate. The set of emails posted in response to Nakamoto's first email, and Nakamoto's response to those emails can be found at: http://www.metzdowd.com/pipermail/cryptography/2008-November/

It seems, from reading Nakamoto's email responses, that Nakamoto was well aware that finer grained detail was required to fully understand and run the bitcoin proposal successfully, and that Nakamoto felt that that detail was best left to the software itself. In answer to questions and critique, Nakamoto writes:

"I had to write all the code before I could convince myself that I could solve every problem, then I wrote the paper." [26]

"I believe I've worked through all those little details over the last year and a half while coding it" [27]

Effectively Nakamoto was saying that the detail is in the software itself. What Nakamoto does not say and can be inferred from his responses is that in order to have written up a paper detailing every last nuance of bitcoin, the paper would have to be as long as the software itself, or longer, as software is compact by comparison to written natural language. As it turned out, when the software was released a few months later, it was 3000 lines long. Papers published in journals are generally limited in size, say 10 pages, such that an exhaustive burden is not put on the peer reviewers and the journal readers in reading through the paper. Nakamoto, in his white paper, released enough information to impress his peers, while keeping the paper short and sweet.

Remarkably, even though never an academic paper that was anonymously peer reviewed for the purposes of seeking publication in an academic journal, since its initial release Nakamoto's paper has been cited over 4000 times [28] in papers that have largely been accepted for publishing by journals. It seems that Satoshi Nakamoto was so sure of his/her/their invention that he/she/they did not bother with seeking approval from others in customary ways, but rather published the paper as a white paper because Nakamoto simply did not care whether the paper was ever published. The paper effectively outlines, *"Here is what we have done and are about to do, and here is broadly how it works"*.

---

[26] Nakamoto email, metzdowd.com mailing list, http://www.metzdowd.com/pipermail/cryptography/2008-November/014832.html, Accessed at Monday, 22 October 2018

[27] Nakamoto email, metzdowd.com mailing list, http://www.metzdowd.com/pipermail/cryptography/2008-November/014863.html, Accessed at Monday, 22 October 2018

[28] Google Scholar, Citation count of Satoshi Nakamoto's "Bitcoin – A peer-to-peer electronic cash system", https://scholar.google.com.au/scholar?hl=en&as_sdt=0%2C5&q=+Bitcoin%3A +A+peer-to-peer+electronic+cash+system&btnG=, referenced at 13th September 2018

What distinguishes Nakamoto is that Nakamoto was not just an academic, but also someone who could program a computer, and actually wrote the first release of the Bitcoin software. In that respect, Nakamoto has been called *"A genius at many levels"*, and that much seems true; especially if we consider genius as taking a range of extant technologies and arranging them in such a novel and unique way as to create something new and unexpected. The *genius* of Nakamoto's invention lies in the detail of how bitcoin works, which we leave to the chapter The Great Scaling Debate, but in essence bitcoin offers a solution to what is known as the Byzantine Generals' Problem which lies at the heart of trusting a public money ledger that everyone has access to and anyone can modify within the set of rules that bitcoin ultimately prescribes.

Of course, Nakamoto targeted the white paper at those who would understand it and appreciate bitcoin; a relatively small group of people who understood cryptography and who were familiar with previous attempts at developing a cryptocurrency, because Nakamoto's bitcoin was not the first attempt at a cryptocurrency. Other cypherpunks had attempted to create cryptocurrencies before Nakamoto and failed.

Nakamoto was intimately aware of previous proposals and attempts to create a viable cryptocurrency. For instance, the first referenced work in Nakamoto's paper is to a work by Wei Dai, where Dai proposes what he called, 'b-money', a proposal that never got off the ground.

What we know of Nakamoto's white paper is that it created excitement and a stir within the cryptocurrency community, to the point that one of the moderators of the mailing list found it necessary to quiet down the commotion. He wrote [29]:

---

[29] Perry Metzger quiets the commotion caused by the release of Nakamoto's bitcoin white paper, netzdowd.com, https://www.mail-archive.com/cryptography@metzdowd.com/msg10012.html, Accessed at Monday, 22 October 2018

```
I'd like to call an end to the bitcoin e-cash
discussion for now a lot of discussion is
happening that would be better accomplished by
people writing papers at the moment rather than
rehashing things back and forth. Maybe later on
when Satoshi (or someone else) writes something
detailed up and posts it we could have another
round of this.

Perry
--
Perry E. Metzger
```

And that is where things were left until Nakamoto came back to the mailing list in January 2009 with an email announcing the release of the bitcoin software.

Nakamoto releases the bitcoin software

In January 2009, mere months after having released his whitepaper, Nakamoto released an announcement that the bitcoin software was ready to use, to the same cryptography group that Nakamoto released her whitepaper to.

If anything can be said most favourably of the success of bitcoin in getting off the ground is that Nakamoto put the effort into realising the bitcoin dream by releasing software to see the vision materialise, and releasing the software to the right group of people, people prepared to help out in getting the bitcoin network established.

Nakamoto's email to the group announcing the software can be seen at http://www.metzdowd.com/pipermail/cryptography/2009-January/014994.html, and it begins:

```
"Announcing the first release of Bitcoin, a new
electronic cash system that uses a peer-to-peer network to
prevent double-spending. It's completely decentralized
with no server or central authority."
```

Whether by accident or design, the software released was called Bitcoin as was the currency, and so to this day, bitcoin is the name of both currency and network.

For many software projects that might have been the end of things. The software was released on an open source repository hosted at a website called Sourceforge (www.sourceforge.net) where anyone can start a new software project and invite others to download the software and to share in responsibility in maintaining the software. Sourceforge and similar code repositories are littered with software projects that have failed to gather any attention, downloads or willing participants offering to provide feedback, bug reports or to help maintain the software.

But Bitcoin was different. The very same day that the Bitcoin software was released, the well known cryptographer Hal Finney downloaded the Bitcoin software and started running it straight away [30]. Years later, Andrea Peterson of The Washington Post would write of the first Bitcoin transaction, 10 bitcoin, being processed in January 2009 and sent from Nakamoto to Finney. Peterson outlined that Finney was enthusiastic about the bitcoin project, reporting bitcoin software bugs to Nakamoto, who fixed them [31].

It is important to a software project that people actually provide feedback on the usage characteristics of the software, including any bugs that the software may contain. Of course, where the processing of money (or cryptocurrency in this case) is concerned, bugs in the software are not acceptable. So the quicker bugs are resolved, the better. In fact, for any critical software system, bugs

---

[30] Forum post of Hal Finney, (19/03/2018), https://bitcointalk.org/index.php?topic=155054.0 , Accessed at Saturday, 20 October 2018

[31] Peterson, Andrea (20/10/2018), "Hal Finney received the first Bitcoin transaction. Here's how he describes it.", The Washington Post, https://www.washingtonpost.com/news/the-switch/wp/2014/01/03/hal-finney-received-the-first-bitcoin-transaction-heres-how-he-describes-it/?noredirect=on&utm_term=.33f117b73003, Accessed at Saturday, 20 October 2018

need to be found and removed from the software before the software is released *live* to the world. In a world where bitcoin (including Bitcoin Cash) represents a market capitalisation reaching into the billions of U.S. dollars, any bug in the software could be catastrophic to the system and the economy it supports.

We know from various sources that the initial bitcoin code was anywhere from 3000 lines of code [32], to 30,000 lines of code [33]. One source puts it at 12,000 lines of code [34], at nearly half way between the two. From my own professional experience, I can safely say that 12,000 lines of quality code would take over a year to write. So Nakamoto's claim that he had been working on the bitcoin software for some time before writing his bitcoin white paper seem legitimate. Nakamoto had released the software only two months after having released the paper.

Software is boring to those who simply wish to use it without understanding it, and the number of lines of code is a boring technicality, but the number of lines of code required to start off the bitcoin project provides an insight into the sheer amount of work that went into writing the software. In a world that is becoming increasingly reliant on software in many areas of life, developers of software are also becoming increasingly aware of their value. This reliance on software developers, and the importance of software development in the bitcoin arena, plays out as we investigate the story of bitcoin further. Enough to say at this stage that Nakamoto was wise enough to invite others to assist

[32] Greg Maxwells self spiel on his involvement with bitcoin, http://diyhpl.us/wiki/transcripts/gmaxwell-bitcoin-selection-cryptography/, Accessed at Thursday, 25 October 2018

[33] Bernard, Zoë (02/12/2017), "Everything you need to know about Bitcoin, its mysterious origins, and the many alleged identities of its creator", Business Insider, https://www.businessinsider.com/bitcoin-history-cryptocurrency-satoshi-nakamoto-2017-12/?r=AU&IR=T/#in-2008-the-first-inklings-of-bitcoin-begin-to-circulate-the-web-1, Accessed at Thursday, 25 October 2018

[34] Forum member on bitcointalk.org discussing bitcoins initial lines of code, https://bitcointalk.org/index.php?topic=289807.0, Accessed at Thursday, 25 October 2018

in developing the bitcoin software, and in doing so, lead the software directly to becoming Bitcoin Cash.

Let us move away from the details and to the abstract vision of bitcoin. What are the core elements of bitcoin as a currency proposed for the world?

The Core Elements of Bitcoin

We know that bitcoin is an electronic currency. That much is easy to conceptualise. But what differentiates bitcoin from other electronic currencies?

While we might not give it much thought, much of the world is already accustomed to using electronic currencies. If you live in a country where you are issued plastic cards that you can swipe in electronic devices to complete a purchase at a store, then you are familiar with electronic currency. Notionally we may correlate the amount of money we transfer to a merchant's account as corresponding to physical paper or metal currency (cash), but mentally we easily understand that not every Australian dollar in existence has a corresponding dollar coin. Indeed most money in countries where electronic currency is widespread is electronic with no physical counterpart. When you borrow $500,000 from the bank to buy a house, the bank manager does not hand you suitcases full of cash; the bank electronically transfers the money to the account of the seller.

So we are familiar with electronic currency. What differentiates bitcoin from other electronic currencies is how it is made and how it is transferred from holder to holder.

NB We speak of Bitcoin Cash here, but the rules are currently the same for Bitcoin Core.

In short, the core elements of bitcoin are:

1. Approximately only 21 million Bitcoin Cash will ever be made. Note, however, that this relates to each bitcoin network. There will be 21 million Bitcoin Cash and 21 million Bitcoin Core.

   The target date for the last Bitcoin Cash (and Core) to be produced is some time in the year 2140, some 120 years from now. The new supply diminishes by half every 4 years, and so bitcoin is inflationary until the year 2140, and then will be deflationary.

   The current rate of Bitcoin Cash creation, in early 2020, is 12.5 Bitcoin Cash issued every 10 minutes on average. The new coins are issued to the individual wallet of someone (or corporation) running the bitcoin software in an effective lottery held between all people running the Bitcoin Cash software. A ticket in that effective lottery is simply running the software, but the more powerful the computer/s running the software, the better chance of winning the lottery.

   Each person or corporation running the software is known as a *miner*, as if mining for gold, which also has a limited supply.

   NB When you run a wallet on your smartphone or computer, that is not running the software that runs the network. Wallets, in general, are not mining. Wallets simply access the network of mining software to effect transactions. Some software has mining capacity and a wallet.

2. Bitcoin transactions are semi-anonymous or offer a level of pseudo-anonymity. People do not have accounts on the bitcoin network but rather, through their wallet, have access to discrete coin values that are allocated to random-looking string of letters and numbers. No personally

identifying information is stored on the distributed bitcoin database.

For this reason, bitcoin can be thought of as an electronic form of cash. People simply transfer bitcoin from one holder to the next. There is no bank through which the transactions take place.

Having said this, there are ways to find out a lot of information about the transactions of any one wallet (balances, transactions etc). For most people accessing that level of detail is not technically feasible, but for law enforcement agencies there are ways and means of gathering information about a wallet.

For instance, if you buy Bitcoin Cash at an exchange and transfer the Bitcoin Cash to your wallet, the flow of money from the exchange, where you may have personally identifying information, to your wallet can be tracked by suitably informed people; regardless of how anonymous you may feel your wallet is.

3. Bitcoin has value by market forces. Bitcoin is no more *backed* by anything than gold is, but similarly has a cost of production. The market determines the value.

4. Anyone with a bitcoin wallet can access the bitcoin network to send or receive bitcoin.

5. The ledger that records the details of which wallet has access to which bitcoin is immutable and a copy of the ledger is held by each mining node within the network.

    Immutable, in this instance, means that the ledger cannot be modified or tampered with it without the rest of the mining nodes knowing that the ledger has been modified. A dishonest player cannot defraud the system without nodes within the network identifying and rejecting the fraud attempt.

This scheme ultimately relies on the majority of the computing power of nodes within the network being honest players who value the network more for the returns the network provides than by trying to defraud the network. As strange as it might seem, 11 years after bitcoin's initial release, this strategy is proving its worth. Nobody has successfully defrauded the bitcoin network. Individual people may have been defrauded, but not the network.

6. Each Bitcoin Cash can be divided into 100,000,000 parts. Each part is now affectionately called a *Satoshi*, in deference to the creator of bitcoin, Satoshi Nakamoto.

7. Miners are rewarded by new bitcoin (currency) issued and transaction fees. That is how the incentive scheme works to keep the network functional.

    Some may think of this as free money, but this is not true. There is a tangible electricity cost to running the software, and the exchange rate of bitcoin often reflects the cost of electricity required to create it.

    Quite obviously bitcoin must have an exchange rate or tangible value greater than the cost of production otherwise many miners would simply not mine bitcoin. Altruism and other factors may entice people to run the software, but the incentive is to create value. History has shown that people are willing to peg value to bitcoin.

    NB This process of rewarding the creator of currency is not new. When governments do this, it is called *seigniorage* and is a form of revenue for a government. For governments this is a form of indirect taxation, as the value of a currency diminishes with inflation, to the detriment of the holders of that currency.

8.   The set of miners around the world form an interconnected network of computers that are effectively *peer-to-peer*. The peer-to-peer architecture makes the whole system very robust and resilient to interference by governments.

   For instance, at the time of writing there are over 2000 copies of Bitcoin Cash software being run on computers throughout the world. If a government wanted to try and shut down Bitcoin Cash, they would have to work with all the governments of the world to try and shut down all 2000 computers to shut down the Bitcoin Cash network, if they could find the computers. This level of political cooperation would be remarkable if it was even possible. It is for this reason that many governments have elected to regulate the cryptocurrency industry rather than try and stamp it out.

These are the core elements of bitcoin. There is a whole raft of considerations that surround those core elements, and we cover those in the chapter, "What is Money?". For now though, we suffice ourselves that the idea of a global cash currency that is highly resistant to government interference was very attractive to many people. Those core elements of bitcoin became more and more popular, and bitcoin became widely accepted as a type of currency.

Ultimately the rise in use of bitcoin as currency led to the realisation of Bitcoin Cash in 2017. Let us look at that journey from 2009 to 2017, because this is where the story hots up.

Bitcoin to 2017 – A Montage

If a movie were to be made of the bitcoin story, at this stage we would move from a blow-by-blow description of who did what and when, to a montage that adequately paints a picture of the major events in bitcoin's history from 2009 to the year 2017 without losing the audience in boring tedium.

Some of the blow-by-blow is very interesting, so I will include snippets here, but to best endeavours I will only put in the most interesting parts of the bitcoin story.

Others get involved in maintaining Bitcoin

In the process of discovering how bitcoin moved from a seminal release of the software in 2009 to the worldwide phenomenon it has become today, it is actually hard work to narrow down exactly who joined Nakamoto, and when, in maintaining the bitcoin software. For the diehard geeks, there are access logs as recorded on the Sourceforge repository (to the now Github repository) where the bitcoin software source code is stored. But the fact that people joined in to help Nakamoto it is not nearly as important or as interesting as that people joined in on Nakamoto's efforts in the first place. What we know today is that Nakamoto did not make all of bitcoin what it is today, she had help along the way. People were genuinely interested in the project and wanted to participate in the project.

Let us look more closely at open source projects and how bitcoin became usable money accepted by people around the world.

Open Source Projects – Bitcoin Core

If you have never had experience with writing computer software it may be difficult to understand what source code is, let alone what an open source project like bitcoin is. Most people would not even care how software is made, just that it is. But with bitcoin you trust your money with software, so the process of how that software is made is important.

While the better part of an entire book might be needed to describe the writing of computer software, it is enough to say that as you read these words (electronically or in print), the words were originally put down electronically and sequentially by myself using a piece of computer software. Ultimately the words in this book were assembled in what is known as a *file*. The file did not do anything but store words. You are reading the contents of that file.

Computer software is pretty much just the same, but software files are used by computers to do something; hopefully something interesting or useful. Computers read files and do something with the information stored in the files. Within software files you assemble words, numbers and characters within those files, and those files ultimately do something when run on a computer. Collectively the files form a *computer program, software code* or simply *code*. In bitcoin's case, those files assemble as a computer program that is run on computers all over the world and, at the time of writing, that software is a large part of the backbone of an economy valued at over $100 billion U.S. dollars.

So of course, the software needs to be maintained and in such a way that its efficiency and security are both of a high standard. If either the efficiency or the security of the bitcoin software were to fail, the economy that it supports would begin to fail, and possibly fail catastrophically.

Open source software is software as an ensemble of files that anyone can download to their computer and inspect its content and structure. You can even view the software online through an internet web browser. This software inspection and sharing happens all the time with bitcoin. Security experts from around the world inspect the software to make sure there is no way that a malicious actor can attack the software while it is running. At the same time, many of those security experts examine the code just to make sure that it runs as expected and will not accidentally rob people of their bitcoin. Some people spend a considerable amount of time doing one or both of those tasks for free. Whether altruistically or as part of some commercial arrangement, whatever their motive, people take an interest in the bitcoin code and make sure it is running the way it should, or provide suggestions for how it could be made better from an efficiency or security perspective.

Other aspects of software that people look at are ease of use, and capabilities. If you are familiar with using computer software, you can probably recall times when you wish the software could do something more for you, or that the software be easier to use. So people review the bitcoin code for ease of use and capability issues as well.

This is all made possible with bitcoin because the software is stored in an *open source repository* on the internet, and where *open* means anyone can come along and look at the software. If you are inclined, you can view the original stream of the bitcoin software at https://github.com/bitcoin/bitcoin on the Github platform, up to the present state of the software.

If you go to that internet domain address, you will see that the software is called "Bitcoin Core". Bitcoin Core is maintained on Github as an *open source project*. Bitcoin Core is not Bitcoin Cash, but is the seminal roots of Bitcoin Cash as initially created by Satoshi Nakamoto up until August 2017.

Let us backtrack on our montage for a second. Who maintains the Bitcoin Core software? How do they maintain the Bitcoin Core software?

Open source projects are an interesting phenomenon. While anyone can view the software, only certain people are allowed to make changes to the software, and fewer people still are allowed to release that software to the world such that people can run the software on computers around the world.

Open source projects have been around, in one way or another, for as long as computer software has been around. Driven largely by a desire for computer software to be free or low-cost, software code has been altruistically shared by people for decades. Some maintain that open source leads to higher quality software, because anyone gets to check the quality of the code. But it was the development of intra-computer networking and the internet that saw a substantial rise in open source projects amalgamating into world-wide endeavours where it became easier for like-minded and goal-oriented people to maintain the code.

So, *how* the Bitcoin Core code is maintained is relatively easy to answer. It is maintained by people from around the world who work together, predominantly on the Github repository platform.

It is the question, *"Who maintains the Bitcoin Core software?"* that is the more interesting. Are these people really like-minded? Are they really goal-oriented, in respect that they share the same goals and visions for code?

This is a more interesting question because group dynamics and politics come into play whenever you have an ensemble of people assembled and interacting within a group, such as an open source project. Bitcoin Cash arose because those who maintain the Bitcoin Core software were so out of tune with those who wanted to see bitcoin grow to having billions of users with low fees in a reasonable timeframe that Bitcoin Cash broke away as its own form of consumer oriented software. Such is the force of politics, market forces and consumer behaviour.

But we are ahead of ourselves…how did Nakamoto get bitcoin off the ground? How did Bitcoin Core get it wrong?

The personnel problems for Satoshi Nakamoto

If Nakamoto wanted bitcoin to be successful, two things were certain. The first is that people had to run the software for it to work, and Nakamoto found no resistance *to* and actually a healthy acceptance *of* the bitcoin software when it was first released; so there was no problem there. Secondly, and probably more importantly, Nakamoto needed for the vision for bitcoin as a whole to be accepted and permeated throughout society if the vision was to become reality.

We have already seen that Nakamoto had pegged bitcoin as a disruptive technology right from the start. Nakamoto knew that electronic peer-to-peer cash would be disruptive to banks and governments. Bitcoin had the potential to forever change how money is issued and created, but it would have been a tall ask for one person to single-handedly change the world all on their own. Nakamoto needed help, and it was forthcoming.

We have seen that Hal Finney jumped in to help out right from the start. But at some stage Nakamoto needed people to help out with maintaining the software until it got to a mature enough state that it could be run with minimal to no changes over time.

In order to do so, Nakamoto invited others to join her on the source code repository, granting access to some people to create new elements of software code.

Within an open source project things are often governed by a meritocracy. Those who show initiative and promise may be invited to join in on the effort. If the quality of their work is up to standard, they may be given more responsibility within the group of people maintaining the code. Of all the roles involved in maintaining code, those who have access to commit new code to the suite of code already extant is an important role. And a more important role again is that role which allows new entrants to participate in the group.

Quite obviously, Satoshi Nakamoto had the governing stake within the open source project when it was first started, but as time moved on, Nakamoto trusted more people to assist in the project.

One would expect that within the process of deciding who would be allowed to make changes to the bitcoin code, was a decision over whether or not those people under consideration shared a common vision for bitcoin. A complex piece of code, incorporating elements from many disciplines in computer science, bitcoin needed to be maintained by not only those who shared the vision, but also with the competencies to make sure that the work they did was of a high quality. But for Nakamoto's vision of bitcoin to be preserved, those who maintained the code needed to share Nakamoto's vision.

Ultimately the decision over who maintains the code is one of trust. The person who ultimately runs the open source project needs to trust in the people who maintain the code.

This became a paradoxical and ironic issue for bitcoin. A currency designed not to require trust in third-parties, such as banks or governments, suddenly needed the trust of a small set of individuals who maintained the code. One slip-up, and the currency could be doomed. One bug, one cracking by a computer hacker and the trust in the currency by its users would be in disarray. The responsibility granted to the people who maintained the code was, and still is, immense. As we have seen, bitcoin in all of its forms commands over $100 billion dollars in asset value. A large component of the responsibility to maintain the value of bitcoin is with the developers of the software.

Enter Gavin Andresen

We know that Nakamoto came to trust one person, Gavin Andresen, and over time granted more permission to Andresen over the maintenance of the bitcoin software. Nakamoto was in charge, but Andresen was increasingly influential within the meritocracy.

Gavin Andresen, unlike Nakamoto, is not a pseudonym but the name of a real and tangible person with, now, quite a well known face and persona. A gently spoken man with intelligence enough to impress Nakamoto, Andresen eventually came to run the Bitcoin Core software project. But now everything is happening at once, our montage is not complete without acknowledging the users of the software and how bitcoin grew in usage, not to mention how Gavin Andresen came to be in charge of the software.

As with all internet phenomenons the swirling rise of that phenomenon is characterised by *the network effect*.

The Network Effect

The network effect is a term that describes the quality of a good or service increasing in value as more people use it [35]. Ironically, rather than individual items of the good or service increasing in value, the value of the collective whole of the good or service increases. For example, with billions of users the internet based Facebook social network platform is worth billions of dollars, but it is free for each of the billions of users to use the network. The collective whole of all those people makes the platform as a whole have a large value.

Bitcoin's network of people running the software grew considerably in the years from 2009 to 2017. Its network effect effectively took off, probably not as fast as other internet phenomenon, but it took off just the same.

---

[35] "The Network Effect", Wikipedia, https://en.wikipedia.org/wiki/Network_effect, Accessed at Friday, 26 October 2018

Most important in the process of bitcoin taking off as a currency was the first currency exchanges, enabling exchange of bitcoin for other denominations and vice versa. The software was released, people started using it, and by late 2009 people wanted to weigh bitcoin's value to fiat currency.

Fiat currency is money declared by a government to be legal tender [36]. People wanted to exchange bitcoin for legal tender.

Exchanges – Bitcoin becomes a tradable currency

Historical facts are sketchy on bitcoin's early days, but it seems that the first exchange rate published for bitcoin was by a website presence known as New Liberty Standard [37] with a price of 1,309.03 Bitcoin's for $1.00 USD on the 5th October 2009, just nine months after bitcoin's initial release. Contrast that price to $344 for one Bitcoin Cash in early 2020, or $8883 for one Bitcoin Core.

Imagine being Satoshi Nakamoto. Nine months earlier Nakamoto had a dream that bitcoin would be adopted and used by people around the world as digital cash, and then, almost out of the blue, people start trading bitcoin as a currency. The feeling must have been exhilarating. Hard work was starting to pay off. A dream had become a reality.

Had anyone bought or sold anything with bitcoin before October 2009? It is hard to say, but we know that on the 22nd of May, 2010, just seven months later again, Laszlo Hanyecz from Florida USA announced on an online forum that he had just bought two

---

[36] Fiat Money, Wikipedia, https://en.wikipedia.org/wiki/Fiat_money, Accessed at Monday, 5 November 2018

[37] Early bitcoin exchange rate, New Liberty Standard, https://web.archive.org/web/20091229132610/http://newlibertystandard.wetpai nt.com/page/Exchange+Rate

pizzas for 10,000 bitcoin (worth $41 US at the time) [38] [39]. What I find more remarkable than the fact that 10,000 bitcoin are worth more than $60 million U.S. dollars at the time of writing is that by May 2010 an online www.bitcointalk.org forum had been established and attracted an active community of people willing to invest their time into exploring the new currency. The forum is still in popular use today, and it seems Nakamoto set up the forum himself, or at least helped to do so. A welcome post from Nakamoto on the forum can be found at https://bitcointalk.org/index.php?topic=5.0 . Nakamoto seems enthusiastic and writes:

"Welcome to the new Bitcoin forum!

The old forum can still be reached here:
http://bitcoin.sourceforge.net/boards/index.php

I'll repost some selected threads here and add updated answers to questions where I can."

Quite obviously Nakamoto knew that she had her audience. People were curious about bitcoin and Nakamoto had answers. It must have been an exciting time. Meeting new people, albeit virtually and over the internet. Sharing knowledge and know-how. Taking the leadership role in a project. Testing Nakamoto's capabilities against other cryptographers, some willing to collaborate, some critics and sceptics. If Nakamoto's dream was to remain a reality things needed to move along with the software, with improvements forthcoming from the core development team…and linking bitcoin to widely used fiat currencies like the U.S. dollar.

---

[38] Hankin, Aaron (22/05/2018), "Bitcoin Pizza Day: Celebrating the $80 Million Pizza Order", Investopia, https://www.investopedia.com/news/bitcoin-pizza-day-celebrating-20-million-pizza-order/, Accessed at Friday, 26 October 2018

[39] Laszlo Hanyecz announces having just bought two pizzas for 10,000 bitcoin on bitcointalk.org, https://bitcointalk.org/index.php?topic=137.0

Of course, Nakamoto did not just know that bitcoin had reached the point where people wanted to buy and sell bitcoin, he encouraged it. In one post on bitcointalk.org, Nakamoto writes:

"LR [Liberty Reserve] and Pecunix have many established exchanges to paper currencies by various payment methods, and a number of vendors accept them as payment, so an exchange link between Bitcoin and LR/Pecunix would give us 2nd-hop access to all that. The possibility to cash out through them would help support the value of bitcoins."

and

"It would be convenient to buy LR/Pecunix with bitcoins rather than through conventional payment methods.

Most customers who convert to LR to buy something would probably ask the seller first if they accept Bitcoin, encouraging them to start accepting it." [40]

And within two months New Liberty Standard (unrelated to Liberty Reserve it seems) starts to exchange bitcoin for U.S. dollars.

People even began exchanging bitcoin for cash via the postal service [41]. Announced within the bitcointalk.org forum, the same thread of conversation announced another bitcoin exchange setup by a user calling themselves BitcoinFX, possibly standing for Bitcoin Forex, where 'Forex' stands for 'Foreign Exchange'.

BitcoinFX finishes the announcement post with:

"We are all getting there Bit by Bit 😊 "

---

[40] Satoshi Nakamoto suggests ways to exchange bitcoin for fiat currency (23/03/2010), bitcointalk.org,
https://bitcointalk.org/index.php?topic=87.msg805#msg805
[41] Bitcoin for cash (and visa versa) via the postal service announced on bitcointalk.org, https://bitcointalk.org/index.php?topic=30.msg1169#msg1169, Accessed at Saturday, 27 October 2018

It had begun.

First Questions of Law

Just two months before bitcoin exchanges started in their seminal form, people started questioning on the forum the legalities of setting up a bitcoin exchange. Questions about regulations, money laundering and money transmitting laws were readily exchanged between people on bitcointalk.org in the month of March 2010 [42].

NewLibertyStandard, who went on to setup the first bitcoin exchange, posted:

"I agree that running an exchange does seem dangerous. I have started extremely small and limited my service so that if I am doing something wrong it will hopefully be so minor that I won't be prosecuted and so that if I am convicted of something the fines will be small enough to hopefully not bankrupt me."

This, in response to:

"Running an exchange seems very dangerous. I would never do it without talking to a lawyer and setting up a LLC [Limited Liability Company]."

A combination of caution, insight and ignorance were to be found all wrapped together in one conversation, with one poster writing:

"I have read about money laundering and it seems that so long as a person is not knowingly laundering money, then the person is not committing the crime."

Even Satoshi Nakamoto joined in on the conversation, seemingly aware of the legal risks of exchanging bitcoin:

---

[42] Discussions about the legality of setting up a bitcoin exchange, bitcointalk.org, https://bitcointalk.org/index.php?topic=69.msg614#msg614, Accessed at Saturday, 27 October 2018

"When there's enough scale, maybe there can be an exchange site that doesn't do transfers, just matches up buyers and sellers to exchange with each other directly, similar to how e-bay works.

To make it safer, the exchange site could act as an escrow for the bitcoin side of the payment. The seller puts the bitcoin payment in escrow, and the buyer sends the conventional payment directly to the seller. The exchange service doesn't handle any real world money.

This would be a step better than e-bay. E-bay manages to work fine even though shipped goods can't be recovered if payment falls through."

Nakamoto was obviously trying to keep things alive. People were starting to ask serious questions of how bitcoin would become usable currency, and the iron was hot.

That was on the 3rd of March, 2010.

By the 23rd of March, 2010, Nakamoto was recommending using the Liberty Reserve, an online money exchange platform that was virtually anonymous and did not have *know your customer* processes in place to gather suitable information about the identity of those exchanging money on the exchange [43].

The trouble there is whether Nakamoto was suitably aware that such a service could readily be used for money laundering. It seems that anyone with the gumption to invent an electronic cash system to usurp banks and government created currency would be well aware of what money laundering was, and the potential for the Liberty Reserve service to be used in that fashion.

Whichever way things are looked at, history shows that starting a new currency is hard and bitcoin faced an uphill battle with

---

[43] Satoshi Nakamoto suggests ways to exchange bitcoin for fiat currency (23/03/2010), bitcointalk.org, https://bitcointalk.org/index.php?topic=87.msg805#msg805

regulation and the law. For example, the Liberty Reserve service was indeed seen by regulators and law enforcement officials as a money laundering exercise. As reported by Charlie McCombie of Coin Telegraph, in 2013 the service was shut down by U.S. investigators, and Arthur Budovsky, who ran the company that ran the service, was arrested for money laundering in 2014. He was subsequently sentenced to 20 years jail [44]!

So posters on bitcointalk.org were right. Running a bitcoin exchange without abiding by laws and regulations was a very precarious occupation.

Compare that with today, where hundreds (if not thousands) of legitimate bitcoin currency exchanges exist around the world. Operating within the law, currency exchanges for bitcoin became a viable business, but it seems none of this would have been possible without the pioneers who got the ball rolling by recognising the value of bitcoin.

It seems incomprehensible that Nakamoto would not have known that there would be pushback from banks and governments over a technology as disruptive as bitcoin. But the fact that bitcoin could not be shut down meant that in many respects, Bitcoin quickly became bigger than Nakamoto and something out of Nakamoto's control.

Things start to get out of control

Whether Nakamoto expected it or not, by late 2010 the chaotic nature of the network effect led to things getting out of Nakamoto's control. Nakamoto was in charge of the project to maintain the bitcoin software, but because people were actually using the bitcoin software and creating new bitcoin, multiple

[44] McCombie, Charlie (10/05/2016), "Bitcoin Predecessor - Liberty Reserve Founder Receives 20-Year Prison Sentence", Coin Telegraph, https://cointelegraph.com/news/bitcoin-predecessor-liberty-reserve-founder-receives-20-year-prison-sentence, Accessed at Saturday, 27 October 2018

minds were working all at once to find ways to use this interesting new currency. The world was not waiting for Nakamoto to decide what was best to do with their bitcoin, people had their own ideas. Some people did not just have ideas as to what they could do with their bitcoin, but had ideas as to what other people could do with their bitcoin.

In December 2010 things started to get hot on the bitcointalk.org forum, and a significant catalyst for discussion was an article published by PC World with the heading, *"Could WikiLeaks Scandal Lead to New Virtual Currency?"* [45].

Wikileaks.org was a website which had upset many powerful people and governments. A site dedicated to releasing information *leaked* to it by whistleblowers, WikiLeaks had released to the world reams of documents that would otherwise be sensitive to organisations and governments. Attracting the ire of governments who labelled whistleblowers traitors rather than conscientious citizens, WikiLeaks was in the crosshairs of law enforcement agencies from around the world.

In a battle between a perceived right to share with the public information of wrong doings and powers that would rather keep such things quiet, the battle took on tactics that are used in general warfare. Take out the supply lines of the enemy and you have a decent chance of winning the battle. And that is what happened.

In 2010 efforts were made to remove WikiLeaks from the internet. The website was attacked with DDOS (Distributed Denial of Service) attacks, which overload a website with so much traffic that if eventually fails to function at all. Dan Nystedt of PC World reported that at one stage WikiLeaks' domain name hosting service removed service from WikiLeaks over the DDOS attacks and www.wikileaks.org could not be accessed at all [46].

---

[45] Thomas, Keir (10/12/2010), "Could the WikiLeaks Scandal Lead to New Virtual Currency?", PC World, https://www.pcworld.com/article/213230/could_wikileaks_scandal_lead_to_ne w_virtual_currency.html, Accessed at Monday, 29 October 2018

On the 4ᵗʰ December 2010 the PayPal internet payment service blocked donations to WikiLeaks altogether, presumably under pressure from governments around the word unhappy with what WikiLeaks was doing. The Reuters news service reported that WikiLeaks' Twitter page simply read "PayPal bans WikiLeaks after US government pressure." [47] A concerted effort was being made to cut of WikiLeaks financial supply.

And 8 days later PC World decided to jump in with their article suggesting that bitcoin was the answer to WikiLeaks woes. The article explains of bitcoin:

"Bitcoins gain their value simply by the fact people are prepared to accept them as payment for services and goods. This sounds weak but this is not entirely dissimilar in nature to the major Fiat currencies such as the Dollar, Euro and Sterling. The only reason we're prepared to accept our wage in dollars is the fact that we know that shops and service providers across the United States (and other countries) are prepared to let us spend it."

…the article then goes on to describe in simplistic terms how bitcoin works.

In any other context this may have been fantastic exposure for Bitcoin. Here was a reputable magazine promoting bitcoin and explaining to people how bitcoin works. Bitcoin had obviously got the attention of someone in a position to promote it, but was this good for Bitcoin?

---

[46] Nystedt, Dan (06/12/2010), "WikiLeaks Vows to Never Say Die With 355 New Websites", PC World, https://www.pcworld.com/article/212507/wikileaks_vows_never_die.html, Accessed at Monday, 29 October 2018

[47] Reuters news report. PayPal suspends payments to WikiLeaks, "PayPal suspends WikiLeaks donations account, Reuters", https://www.reuters.com/article/wikileaks-paypal-idUSN0415723720101204, Accessed at Monday, 29 October 2018

It seems that the debate had actually started one month earlier on the bitcointalk.org forum and somehow had percolated its way up to mainstream media. Someone wrote on the forum in November a full month before PC World's WikiLeaks/Bitcoin article:

"Hey,

I wanted to send a letter to Wikileaks about Bitcoin since unfortunately they've had several incidents where their funds have been seized in the past.

...
Anyone know where to send a message to them?"

And that was it. That was enough to start a thread of conversation that gained over 100 replies and replies to replies. Seen as an opportunity and a threat at the same time, opinions came thick and fast.

"Yeah this may be good for wikileaks, but not nocessarily good for Bitcoin. If bitcoin becomes publicly associated with wikileaks before going semi-mainstream, then it will be viewed by the "ruling class" (read: US government) as a tool for doing money laundering and another "gray" buisnesses.

This may make bitcoin be considered by governments as a serious threat, and they will start fighting it too soon, holding back mainstream adoption.

Of course i know that they (governments) will start fighting bitcoin at some point, but the later, the better. If we go mainstream first, then such efforts will be probably futile, and BTC will probably be unstoppable without shutting down whole internet." [48]

Hitting on the fact that to shutdown Bitcoin one would have to shut down practically all of the peers in the network, this post captures the essence of Bitcoin. With enough peers, to shut down

---

[48] Talk on Bitcointalk.org re WikiLeaks taking donations in bitcoin, www.bitcointalk.org, https://bitcointalk.org/index.php?topic=1735.0, Accessed at Monday, 5 November 2018

bitcoin you would have to shut down the internet before Bitcoin was shut down; an almost impossibility.

But more than that, the post captures the essence of an early Bitcoin. Of course these people were creating their own currency. Of course governments of the world would dislike that. Of course being associated with WikiLeaks would taint Bitcoin.

But what did anyone truly expect? It was never the case that any bank or government would stand up and say, *"By all means, create a globally used currency! Usurp the banks and the U.S. dollar standard! Why would we care?"*

Bitcoin users already knew they were playing with fire, but they also knew that the technology was unstoppable. One anonymous poster was not so sure:

"Contrary to popular opinion it is not illegal to create your own currency. If they try to claim there is something illegal in the mere act of transferring value or bits of data they will look ridiculous."

In what country? In what capacity is the currency operating? Legal tender? Is this true of any country?

The debate had begun, and the perceived gravity of the effect of Bitcoin on the world is captured in one post:

"Why do i feel more and more convinced that the internet era will end governments in the form we know them ?"

Clearly these people knew that Bitcoin was world changing. The history of currency was being rewritten, and the open forum captures, for the entire world to see, its beginning...

"If you're reading this, you're part of the vanguard building the new economy and the new world. Mainstream acceptance will come by weight of numbers and via network effects."

This sentiment was shared by others on the forum, with one post culminating in…

"Basically, bring it on. Let's encourage Wikileaks to use Bitcoins and I'm willing to face any risk or fallout from that act." [49]

The trouble with that sentiment was that others were well aware of the potential repercussions to Bitcoin if the governments of the world chose to fight back against populist money creation. Jeff Garzik, who went on to co-found a company based on the technology Nakamoto brought to the world, responded harshly…

"Thanks for being willing to helpfully impose risk upon others. For people who are just starting to build businesses on bitcoin, this could be devastating to their new business."

Wikileaks is the enemy of major world powers right now, with many influential elites feeling that Assange committed an act of war against the United States, or, at a minimum, irrevocably disrupted world affairs. This is not some mailing list discussion or theoretical exercise; there are very real, very powerful organizations actively targetting [sic] wikileaks' network infrastructure, organizational infrastructure, and most importantly, financial infrastructure.

It is extraordinarily unwise to make bitcoin such a highly visible target, at such an early stage in this project. There could be a lot of "collateral damage" in the bitcoin community while you make your principled stand."

Already people could see the business potential of Nakamoto's invention and wanted nothing to do with the shady area that WikiLeaks operated in. Already people were aware that governments were not entirely to be toyed with so flippantly. In retrospect, though, how could anyone have seen that Bitcoin's presence as global uncensored electronic cash would ever make it

---

[49] "Bring it on"…WikiLeaks and Bitcoin, www.bitcointalk.org, https://bitcointalk.org/index.php?topic=1735.msg26876#msg26876

to the world stage without first having been a challenge to the powers that had controlled money for so long?

Having probably sat back and watched the debate proceed up to this point, reserving judgement until the implications of WikiLeaks accepting donation payment in Bitcoin set in, Nakamoto finally put his two bits forth...

"No, don't "bring it on".

The project needs to grow gradually so the software can be strengthened along the way.

I make this appeal to WikiLeaks not to try to use Bitcoin. Bitcoin is a small beta community in its infancy. You would not stand to get more than pocket change, and the heat you would bring would likely destroy us at this stage." [50]

It must have been a sinking feeling for Nakamoto that her project was slipping away from her grasp, and in a manner which jeopardised the future of the currency. In another month Bitcoin would have been 2 years old, slowly getting off the ground, and here were people acting with what the cautious saw as reckless abandon.

It is hard to know what Nakamoto was truly feeling at the time, but the sense of community is in the word *us,* and one can imagine the pressure Nakamoto was under... *"the heat you would bring would likely destroy us"*. Nakamoto was well aware that Bitcoin was at its first tipping point. A garage project with a small following was potentially about to get its first full exposure to a bigger world. From the secrecy of the cypherpunks, Bitcoin was now being exposed.

And then it happened, despite efforts to dissuade people from tying Bitcoin to WikiLeaks. Someone posted that PC World had published their article, publicly calling the rally cry for Bitcoin to

---

[50] Nakamoto says, "No, don't 'bring it on'", www.bitcointalk.org, https://bitcointalk.org/index.php?topic=1735.140

be the saviour of WikiLeaks.

"I guess it's too late now.

The words bitcoin and wikileaks have appeared in the same headline in pc world just now.

Search google news for the word bitcoin now." [51]

Nakamoto wrote…

"It would have been nice to get this attention in any other context. WikiLeaks has kicked the hornet's nest, and the swarm is headed towards us." [52]

The sense of high drama in Nakamoto's words is palpable. Or is it a sense of realism? In some sense Nakamoto's words were prophetic, Bitcoin went on to create a storm that has affected nearly every government in the world. Nakamoto had a real sense that what the Bitcoin cypherpunks and hangers-on were doing was dangerous. The *hornets* were obviously law enforcement officials from around the world who would come to see Bitcoin as a dangerous technology, capable of disrupting well established power positions, especially when it came to the ability to track payments around the world, stop payments and seize bank accounts when deemed fit. Nakamoto had introduced this disruptive technology, and we know from history that *us* really meant *me*. As the inventor and chief protagonist of Bitcoin, the hornets would have been after Nakamoto. We get a real sense of Nakamoto's self induced paranoia by what Nakamoto did next.

---

[51] Announcement that PC World had published an article on Bitcoin being the potential saviour for WikiLeaks, www.bitcointalk.org, https://bitcointalk.org/index.php?topic=1735.160, Accessed at Tuesday, 30 October 2018

[52] Nakamoto reacts to PC World's article on Bitcoin being the saviour of WikiLeaks, www.bitcointalk.org, https://bitcointalk.org/index.php?topic=2216.msg29280#msg29280, Accessed at Tuesday, 30 October 2018

Details are a bit sketchy at this stage, and it is incredible that much of the history of Bitcoin is available online for anyone to find, but we know enough to piece together Nakamoto's movements between December 2010 and April 2011. Nakamoto orchestrated his own disappearance.

Casually Nakamoto wrote on bitcointalk.org on 12th December 2010…

"There's more work to do on DoS, but I'm doing a quick build of what I have so far in case it's needed, before venturing into more complex ideas." [53]

Nakamoto was saying goodbye to his followers. Effectively saying, "I am just tidying up here, before I leave. I am moving on to more complex ideas."

And with that Nakamoto was gone. He never wrote on the bitcointalk forum again. Bitcoin was being left to its own devices, and if the hornets came looking, Nakamoto would be nowhere to be found.

How could Satoshi Nakamoto leave Bitcoin?

It almost sounds like a rhetorical question of woe, *"How could Nakamoto leave Bitcoin?"* Here was someone who had profoundly shaped a new technology and on the verge of shaping history, and she was disappearing. How could Nakamoto do that?

It is not just a rhetorical question though. There are the practicalities of leaving a project in good shape.

Nakamoto may have disappeared from the bitcointalk forum, but Nakamoto still communicated with select people via email for the

---

[53] Nakamoto sends a cryptic goodbye on the bitcointalk forum, www.bitcointalk.org, https://bitcointalk.org/index.php?action=profile;u=3;sa=showPosts;start=0, Accessed at Tuesday, 30 October 2018

next few months. In particular, Nakamoto had warmed to Gavin Andresen who had been developing code for bitcoin. And it is to Andresen that Nakamoto left the reins.

As Andresen puts it, Nakamoto asked him if it was okay to put Andresen's name as one of the developers of Bitcoin on the front page of the www.bitcoin.org website, which Nakamoto had setup even before releasing his white-paper and which is still used to promote Bitcoin to this day [54]. Accepting the request, Nakamoto updated the site, and then, seemingly *when the time was right*, removed Satoshi Nakamoto's name as the lead developer and substituted Andresen's name instead. When was that right time?

It was all carefully orchestrated. As the New Year broke, 2011 proved to be an extraordinary year for bitcoin and the world of technology in general, especially when it came to technology's impact on society.

Have you ever been in a job where others around you have been retrenched or fired, and there has not been time for a decent hand-over of information in the mind of those who have left? Have they left a job half-done and you need to pick up the pieces? If not, imagine a teacher leaving the classroom and the students to their own devices. Suddenly things are all up to you. The teacher usually nominates someone to be in charge while they are gone, but half the time that does not save the situation…chaos ensues.

The network effect pretty much ensured that all things Bitcoin would become chaotic, with different forces operating all at the same time. What is most interesting of this time however is that Nakamoto seems to have left Bitcoin at just the right time.

By April 2011 Nakamoto had left Andresen in charge of the software code on the software repository, and it had become known that Andresen was now a key player in the Bitcoin arena.

---

[54] Bitcoin documentary, "Banking on Bitcoin", https://www.youtube.com/watch?v=uPBIp-QO6UM, Accessed at Monday, 5 November 2018

Andresen was still communicating with Nakamoto, but to the bitcointalk forum, Andresen was now public property.

In April 2011 Andresen posted something on the bitcointalk forum that would forever alter the Bitcoin conversation. It is best left to Andresen's own words...[55]

"I want to get this out in the open because it is the kind of thing that will generate conspiracy theories: I'm going to give a presentation about Bitcoin at CIA [The USA's Central Intelligence Agency] headquarters in June at an emerging technologies conference for the US intelligence community.

I accepted the invitation to speak because the fact that I was invited means Bitcoin is already on their radar, and I think it might be a good chance to talk about why I think Bitcoin will make the world a better place. I think the goals of this project are to create a better currency, create a more competitive and efficient international payment system, and give people more direct control over their finances. And I don't think any of those goals are incompatible with the goals of government.

I'm only very slightly worried that talking about bitcoin at the CIA will increase the chances they'll try to do something we don't want them to do. I think accepting their invitation and being open about exactly what bitcoin is will make it less likely they'll see it as a threat.

PS: Full disclosure: I'll be paid a one-time fee of $3,000 to cover expenses and pay me for my time. I don't want any "Gavin is on the CIA's payroll" rumors to get started, either...

As always, comments and questions and discussion welcome. I'd really rather not hear any conspiracy theories about how they'll secretly implant a mind-control chip in my head while I'm there, though...."

---

[55] Gavin Andresen is invited to speak with the CIA about Bitcoin, www.bitcointalk.org, https://bitcointalk.org/index.php?topic=6652.0, Accessed at Wednesday, 31 October 2018

The post speaks for itself. The dipole between theory that Bitcoin would benefit the world and at the same time cause havoc for law enforcement agencies was manifest, as was Nakamoto's prophecy that the hornets would come swarming. It is a credit to Gavin Andresen how coolly he managed the situation and how polite the CIA had been in inviting Mr Andresen to fill them in on Bitcoin.

But where had this come from? What had triggered this event? WikiLeaks had not yet taken up Bitcoin donations. What was the driver?

The Silk Road

Well, it is simple really. The Sydney Morning Herald newspaper of Australia reported in June of 2011 that in February 2011 a black market website offering anonymous sale of drugs and munitions for bitcoin had opened on the dark web (websites available through special web browsers offering a high degree of privacy and anonymity) [56].

And on 1st March 2011, a pseudonymous poster called *silkroad* on bitcointalk.org wrote:

"Hi everyone,

Silk Road is into it's third week after launch and I am very pleased with the results. There are several sellers and buyers finding mutually agreeable prices, and as of today, 28 transactions have been made!" [57]

---

[56] Norrie, J. Asher, M., (11/06/2011), Drugs bought with virtual cash, Sydney Morning Herald, https://www.smh.com.au/technology/drugs-bought-with-virtual-cash-20110611-1fy0a.html, Accessed at Wednesday, 31 October 2018

[57] Silk Road announced on bitcointalk.org, www.bitcointalk.org, https://bitcointalk.org/index.php?topic=3984.0, Accessed at Wednesday, 31 October 2018

The service took bitcoin payments into escrow; suppliers shipped goods to customers via the mail.

The post thread itself goes on for page after page, post after post. The post had a profound effect on the nascent bitcoin community.

One poster commented:

"I'm afraid to even be posting here 🙂

brb [be right back], a black van just pulled up and two men in suits are at the door..."

Bitcoin had opened the door to anonymous cash payment for drugs and munitions on the internet, without having to use a credit card or bank account. The whole idea that bitcoin was as good as cash was coming to fruition. Bitcoin exchanges were in full swing. People could substitute their fiat currency for bitcoin and shop with bitcoin anywhere bitcoin was accepted with relative privacy. The public ledger of bitcoin held no personally identifying information and so long as nobody knew who owned a wallet, transactions with bitcoin were anonymous.

So it is no surprise that only a month later the CIA came knocking. What is surprising is just how quickly they came knocking. These were not slouches finding out about bitcoin years after criminal activity started with bitcoin, these were people with their finger on the pulse.

And where was Nakamoto during all of this? Well and truly in the background. Gavin Andresen reports that on emailing Nakamoto that he was invited to speak with the CIA, that was the last that he heard from Nakamoto.

Another key and early bitcoin developer, Mike Hearn, is probably the last person to have contact with Nakamoto (as Nakamoto). Hearn was corresponding with Nakamoto via email and asked, among other things, if Nakamoto was going to return to bitcointalk. Nakamoto merely responded:

"I've moved on to other things. It's in good hands with Gavin and everyone." [58]

And that was it. Nakamoto was gone for good.

But where was Bitcoin?

The introduction of the Silk Road black market service brought a serious real-world use case to Bitcoin. Before long the price of a Bitcoin rose to $30 per bitcoin on exchanges. People were actively using Bitcoin for criminal activity, and this soon became one of the major uses of the currency.

The software development effort itself was left with Gavin Andresen in charge, and it seems that no effort was made by law enforcement to shut down the project. What could anyone do anyway? The source code for the project was out in the open, the software decentralised; any attempt to shut down Bitcoin would have seen just another cryptocurrency take its place. The genie was well and truly out of the bottle.

In June of 2011 WikiLeaks finally started accepting donations of bitcoin to help fund their efforts. While having initially respected Nakamoto's request for WikiLeaks not to be associated with Bitcoin, the organisation had a change of heart. Observing that the Silk Road had effectively increased the price of Bitcoin and helped established the currency, it is hard to imagine why Bitcoin would not be then used by WikiLeaks. Bitcoin was perfect for their needs. Where governments sought to censure WikiLeaks, enter a currency that could not be censured. The Forbes news network helped break the story to world. [59]

---

[58] Mike Hearn's last emails with Satoshi Nakamoto, https://pastebin.com/syrmi3ET, Accessed at Monday, 5 November 2018
[59] Greenburg A. (14/06/2011), "WikiLeaks Asks For Anonymous Bitcoin Donations", Forbes, https://www.forbes.com/sites/andygreenberg/2011/06/14/wikileaks-asks-for-anonymous-bitcoin-donations/#21c13d864f73, Accessed at Monday, 5

Nakamoto's initial regret that the attention that Bitcoin was getting was from all the wrong places was now a cemented reality. Bitcoin was well and truly linked to criminal activity and shady dealings. The whole cryptocurrency market was both new and a grey area under law at the same time. As we have noted, it is hard to see that Bitcoin would have had any other start in life. There is not a government on earth that would have welcomed Bitcoin with open arms. But here it was.

The montage roundup

History has shown that Bitcoin survived its shady beginnings and even thrived. Six years does not seem that long a time, but it is almost an eternity in the information technology game. In the six years to 2017:

1. More exchanges opened around the world;
2. Governments formulated legislation around cryptocurrencies;
3. Bitcoin came to be used for legal and illegal purposes;
4. People speculated on the price of bitcoin rising relative to fiat currencies;
5. Legitimate businesses started forming around Bitcoin;
6. Internet payment processors began integrating with Bitcoin; and
7. Other cryptocurrencies and Bitcoin survived.

Things did not end well for Silk Road or its founder, Ross Ulbricht. Ulbricht was eventually prosecuted for his involvement in the Silk Road and sentenced to two life sentences, with no possibility of parole. The Forbes news network was there again to report the story as it became global news [60].

November 2018
[60] Vinton, K. (29/05/2015), "Silk Road Creator Ross Ulbricht Sentenced To Life In Prison", Forbes, https://www.forbes.com/sites/katevinton/2015/05/29/ulbricht-sentencing-silk-road/#21b4c8e5c6e7, Accessed at Monday, 5 November 2018

WikiLeaks still accepts Bitcoin payments to this day [61].

What is important to our story is that the Bitcoin software was left in charge of Gavin Andresen and other programmers. Nakamoto felt that he had left Bitcoin in good hands. That may well have been the case, and for some time, but beyond the politics and economics of a new currency is the story of what happens when a computer software project is hijacked and taken over by those who do not necessarily believe in the politics and economics that spawned the creation of the currency in the first place. A coup eventually ousted Andresen and others left bitcoin in disgust.

Before that happened, though, the Bitcoin software came to be called Bitcoin Core to differentiate the software, by name, from the currency, the coup happened and then Bitcoin became Bitcoin Cash and Bitcoin Core. Ours is the story of Bitcoin Cash, but first let us look at what is Bitcoin Core.

---

[61] WikiLeaks still accepts Bitcoin as donation payment, www.wkileaks.org, https://shop.wikileaks.org/donate, Accessed at Monday 5 November, 2018

What is Bitcoin Core?

Basically, Bitcoin Core is the cryptocurrency that Bitcoin Cash broke away from because of ideological differences about how Bitcoin should be run. The split occurred on the 1st August 2017. As we have seen, there was a lot of bitcoin history between 2009 and 2017.

More specifically Bitcoin Core is the name of the software that runs the network of the cryptocurrency that has the ticker symbol BTC at cryptocurrency exchanges around the world. Bitcoin Core is a variant of the Bitcoin software. That is, you can track the price of BTC against a fiat currency, such as the U.S. dollar, on a range of websites and exchanges. When you purchase Bitcoin Core through an exchange, you purchase the currency referenced as BTC. Bitcoin Cash, on the other hand, is referenced by the exchange ticker symbol, BCH. The price of Bitcoin relative to other currencies is driven by market forces and where hundreds of cryptocurrency exchanges around the world offer Bitcoin for sale. In those countries where cryptocurrencies are legal tender, these exchanges are reflective of currency exchanges that you encounter at airports. In as much as Australian dollars are referenced by the ticker symbol AUD, Bitcoin Core is referenced by the symbol, BTC.

The original bitcoin software was renamed Bitcoin Core in 2014 in an attempt to disambiguate the network software from the currency [62]. That attempt does not seem to have been entirely successful up until recently, as people still referred to the bitcoin network and the currency as bitcoin. But it is a fortuitous distinction to have been made, because with the original bitcoin network having now been split into Bitcoin Core and Bitcoin Cash it is easier to understand what that distinction is. Both are offshoots of the original bitcoin software and network, each with their own characteristics.

---

[62] https://bitcoin.org/en/release/v0.9.0#how-to-upgrade

At the time of writing, BTC has the largest market capitalisation (some U.S. $180 billion), and represents nearly 60% of all money committed to cryptocurrency assets. This is in stark contrast to the 100% market share Bitcoin Core started with in 2009, and the nearly 98% market share that BTC held in 2016.

Many argue that the ideology of those in charge of the BTC network and management of the Bitcoin Core software are to blame for that loss of market dominance. Either way it is looked at, the marketing of Bitcoin Core has arguably been very poor with people having voted with their feet and left the network.

Would there ever have been a split of bitcoin if the people managing the BTC software had been more responsive to the needs of those that started Bitcoin Cash? This is something we will dive into in the next chapter. Realistically, there are many reasons for the loss of market share of Bitcoin Core, including the proliferation of other cryptocurrencies. Of course there are also other bitcoins, such as Bitcoin Gold and Bitcoin Diamond.

First, let us look at why Bitcoin Cash split from Bitcoin Core.

The primary reason for the split from BTC to form Bitcoin Cash was that those in control of the BTC software code-base, and subsequent network, seemed to make it clear that Bitcoin should represent a store of value (i.e. act as digital form of gold), rather than be a readily used currency. The *store of value* quality of Bitcoin seems to have gained precedence over a *readily used currency* quality because the price of Bitcoin did increase over time given the relative scarcity of Bitcoin, but the Bitcoin software was structured such that with increased popularity so too would the cost per transaction (to the spender/sender of bitcoin) increase. So what would it matter if those store-of-value gains outweighed transaction costs? Early speculators in Bitcoin made fortunes when they held the currency for a long enough period of time. For instance Jordan Bishop of Forbes reported in 2017 that a man had made U.S. $25million profit from simply holding onto

Bitcoin acquired at a much earlier date when Bitcoin exchanged at low cost to the U.S. dollar [63]. Reducing the cost of doing business with Bitcoin, governed by the cost of each transaction, took lower precedence with those in charge of maintaining the Bitcoin Core software and the miners running the network. Miners and holders could make good money as the network effect increased the value of the bitcoin network and each bitcoin.

Decisions were made to actually throttle bitcoin by effectively increasing transaction fees if the network became too popular, so that *anyone* could run the Bitcoin Core software and not suffer data transfer and storage costs by having many transactions to handle.

As with most things in life, it was not quite as simple as that, but a retrospective on Bitcoin Core is only accurate if the reality that high price transaction fees was the outcome of a decision made by BTC developers not to scale Bitcoin Core to meet high and increasing demand. If that decision were not made Bitcoin Cash would never have split from Bitcoin Core. This became known as the Great Scaling Debate and is ultimately why the split occurred.

The decision to throttle the bitcoin network seems to have been a critical mistake, as the brain trust of academics, software developers and marketing elite now seem to have moved to Bitcoin Cash and other currencies. The reason for this is that Bitcoin Cash proponents argue that bitcoin will never reach mass adoption without low transaction fees and bitcoin will never be a store of value without mass adoption. That is, the network effect works also in reverse. A currency is virtually worthless if nobody uses or accepts the currency.

---

[63] Bishop, Jordan (07/07/2017), "Meet The Man Travelling The World On $25 Million Of Bitcoin Profits", Forbes, https://www.forbes.com/sites/bishopjordan/2017/07/07/bitcoin-millionaire/#242501446261, Accessed at Monday, 5 November 2018

We tackle the scaling debate as we progress through this book, but enough to say that at one point in 2017 it cost U.S. $50 per transaction on the Bitcoin Core network, effectively driving away any notion of a readily usable peer-to-peer electronic cash system and leading to a seismic crash of the exchange price of Bitcoin Core, not long after Bitcoin Cash broke from Bitcoin Core. News BTC, a bitcoin news network, reported on the story [64].

To anyone looking in on Bitcoin, it seems inconceivable that those in charge of maintaining a currency would not wish for ready use of the currency, but the evidence supports that viewpoint. We cover the split and brain drain as we move through the book, but enough to say that when people spoke of Bitcoin in the past, the predominantly spoke of just Bitcoin Core. Now the waters are irreversibly muddied and market forces will determine winners and losers in the space.

Take away - To become a widely used currency, the Bitcoin Cash narrative is that transactions need to be fast, reliable and cheap *and* Bitcoin Cash must also be a store of value. This seems to be a winning strategy to the author's mind. It makes sense. An electronic currency can have both qualities.

Recall that the very first objection that Nakamoto received to his bitcoin paper was a suggestion that a peer-to-peer network would find it very difficult to handle a large throughput of transactions[65]. Debate raged in the Bitcoin Core community from that point on and for years to come, as to how to scale Bitcoin Core to handle the throughput of transactions required for a global electronic cash transaction platform.

---

[64] Bintinx, JP, (22/12/2017), "Bitcoin's Transaction fee exceeds $50 as Network Issues Remain", News BTC, https://www.newsbtc.com/2017/12/22/bitcoins-average-transaction-fee-surpasses-50-network-issues-remain/, Accessed at Monday, 5 November 2018
[65] First objection to Nakamoto's Bitcoin paper, www.metzdowd.com, http://www.metzdowd.com/pipermail/cryptography/2008-November/014814.html, Accessed at Monday, 5 November 2018

The details are technical and are covered in the next chapter, but what seems to have happened is that rather than preferring to make money from many low transaction fees, Bitcoin Core proponents preferred to simply raise the cost of transactions the more transactions there were to process and effectively throttle the network. That would stop scaling in its tracks. And throttle the network they did, in more ways than one…

At the beginning of 2017, Bitcoin Core had more than 80% market dominance over all other cryptocurrencies. Bitcoin Cash broke away from Bitcoin Core in August 2017, and by the end of 2017, Bitcoin Core only held 38% of market share. That has steadily come back to around 60%, but at an undeniably high cost [66]. As transaction fees on the Bitcoin Core network reached US $50 per transaction payment integrators dropped Bitcoin Core from their payment gateways. Tanaya Macheel of Tearsheet, a financial news outlet, reported the matter and argued in a published article that '*bitcoin was never a good payment mechanism*' and should rather be '*a store of value*' [67]. If that is not a currency being throttled, I am unsure what is.

The debate over whether Bitcoin could scale had dragged on for years, with the creators of the Bitcoin Cash currency finally called it quits, forged their own path, and ultimately formed their own currency; Bitcoin Cash. Now it is impossible to talk of Bitcoin without distinguishing which Bitcoin you are talking about. Bitcoin Core, if one is to ask, is simply one form of Bitcoin.

Competition between currencies is key

---

[66] Bitcoin Core dominance charts, www.coinmarketcap.com, https://coinmarketcap.com/charts/, Accessed at Monday, 5 November 2018

[67] Macheel, Tanaya (25/01/2018), "Why bitcoin should be a 'store of value'", Tearsheet, https://www.tearsheet.co/blockchain/why-bitcoin-should-be-a-store-of-value, Accessed at Monday, 5 November 2018

A recurring theme presented by proponents of Bitcoin Cash is that healthy competition between digital and fiat currencies is positive and will lead to currencies that better serve people.

When it comes to competition between Bitcoin Cash and Bitcoin Core, it can be taken for granted that the aim of Bitcoin Cash is to become the dominant currency. To achieve that aim there are quite obviously many hurdles to surmount, with Bitcoin Core still being the dominant cryptocurrency in terms of exchange price at the time of writing; achieving the mind share of people being key amongst those hurdles.

The way that Bitcoin Cash has initially differentiated itself from Bitcoin Core is to develop a network that can manage millions of transactions per day and at a very low fee per transaction. While a seemingly obvious way to attract commerce and adoption, the effort required by the developers of Bitcoin Cash and its subsequent promoters was extraordinarily large. The precursory politics behind that battle is what we cover when we explore The Great Scaling Debate later in this book.

Interlude

The World Wide Web on the internet is a wonderful thing. You can jump from site to site as your whim takes you. A book is a little bit different. Generally books are read from beginning to end.

In writing this book, however, I have had quite a significant challenge. Recount The Great Scaling Debate before talking more about money and cryptocurrencies in general, or do we explore the concepts of what is money first?

The Great Scaling Debate is quite an interesting story, and that story encapsulates the essence of this book…that **you must trust the team behind a currency in order to trust the currency and cryptocurrencies are not trustless as some may have you believe**.

That story, however, takes a plunge into the technicalities of how Bitcoin works which may not be appealing to those who just want to use a cryptocurrency without knowing all the details. You may also first want to know how a cryptocurrency can be regarded as a form of currency in the first place.

In my book, customers come first. So the next few chapters outline *What is Money?* and the vision of *'Bitcoin Cash - 'Sound money to the world'* , before going into the technicalities of bitcoin.

For those who want to dive into the dirt of how bitcoin works and how The Great Scaling Debate came about, jump a few chapters ahead and then come back here.

What is Money?

If you are like just about everybody else, then you do not give much thought as to where money comes from or indeed as to what money really is. Money is just something that most of us have to work for, and in the past it came from governments. Right? Well, mostly yes, on both counts. But if you have never asked yourself where governments get money from, then you are in for a ride which may propel you to better understanding the reason why cryptocurrencies came about in the first place, and possibly drive you to adopting cryptocurrency in your life.

The history of money is thousands of years old, and intuitively we understand that money probably first began as bargaining chips for payment of goods and services exchanged between people. Shell money is one such example of items used as payment, where sea shells were used as a medium of exchange [68]. It is easy to imagine that hard to find sea shells were worth more than others, and some measure of work was required to find and collect them. Rarity of particular shells added to their value, especially if the shells were traded inland from the coast. Intuitively this is easy to understand, and a key word in the narrative is that each shell has a measure of *worth*.

What is worth and how is it measured? With money and the goods traded with money, intuitively we all realise that worth is the value that any one person puts on the money and goods and services traded for that money. I like that bowl of milk; I will give you 10 seas shells for that bowl of milk. No, you say, I want 20 sea shells. Ah! A tough bargain. But the point is clear; the worth of money is subjective even when collectively we might otherwise say that the average bowl of milk is worth only 5 sea shells.

---

[68] Sell Money, Wikipedia, https://en.wikipedia.org/wiki/Shell_money , Accessed at Saturday, 18 January 2020

You could go in circles forever defining worth if you tried. What is worth? Well it is the value you put on something. Then what is value? Well it is whatever worth you put on something. And round you go. At some stage you have to rely on your own intuition as to what value and worth are, and that intuition can extend to evaluating the consensus of everyone else's worth placed on an item. These things are at the heart of understanding money. Money has worth because the general consensus is that it does, or until such time as it doesn't, as the case may be. Shell money certainly lost favour over time and shells once possibly worth a fortune are now worth relatively little.

Nobody knows for certain when people started bargaining with token objects separate from actual commodities traded (e.g. bartering a cow for baskets of wheat as opposed for a piece of gold), all we know is that independently around the world, many societies settled on some form of token as a form of settlement for a trade. In some societies it was seas shells, in others it was wheel shaped stones, in others it was lumps of hard to find metals. What we know is that the token of exchange has become more sophisticated over time, and, it seems, mostly so that counterfeit tokens are harder to produce as to somehow keep things honest. Under a shell money system, if I could miraculously manifest lots of sea shells out of thin air, and not have to work at all for them, then suddenly I would have a great deal of money and fall foul of others, not to mention effectively devaluing the money because there would suddenly be a lot of it around.

This leads us to an aspect of money which is almost universal in all societies. Money is, in general, relatively scarce and difficult to come by. If money is a scarce commodity this lends to the money holding value and helps create an economy where people strive to accumulate money such that they can purchase the things that they want, but also such that they do not need to do as much if they are the holders of a proportionally larger share of money than others in the economy or have enough of it for their needs.

The story of money is rich and complex, and I hesitate to provide a historic blow by blow account of the history of money in this book because intuitively you understand a lot about money already and have some feel for its history already. But there are things about money in today's modern societies that you may not know, and which may shock you to the core once you know and understand those things.

My first introduction to the intrigue of money came about when I was about ten years old. My first cousin, who was only abut twelve at the time, took me aside and told me the story of money as it works in most of the western world as he had somehow learned. He said, "Did you know that banks do not have to have the money they lend you in their account when they lend it to you? Do you know that they just create that money out of thin air?" Quite obviously I was shocked, but before I could get a word in, he went on to tell me that each bank need only have about 10% of all money that they lend out as real money in their accounts, and the rest of the money they just create out of thin air. He said the banks could purchase things that he called bankers bonds from a reserve bank which the reserve bank paid interest on. He said that the reserve bank did not really have any money, but the government effectively create the money out of thin air along with the reserve bank, and the money is just past down the line. "I am going to get my hands on some of these bankers bonds" he said. His naming of the financial instruments in play may not have been right, but he was right about what he called *the system*. It is called the "Fractional Reserve Banking System".

I was, of course, a little bit marvelled as a ten year old as to how he knew so much about banking at such a young age. I am not sure if he has ever got his hands on any of these 'bankers bonds', but he sure was keen. Money for nothing seemed like a good idea to him at the time. He seemed to think that much secrecy obscured the whole enterprise and you had to be someone in the know to get in on the act. This much, it turns out, is very true to this day.

To be honest, I did not give it much more thought after that. My position in life is that if you are going to be rich, that is something you are going to do anyway, by volition of who you are. But as I got older, and as from time to time I found money hard to come by, my thoughts went back to that conversation.

In writing this book I have dived deep into understanding the fractional reserve system. It seems to me that it is critical that all people on Earth who use money should know how that money comes about. More importantly, I feel that it is important that people know why their savings are eroded by a targeted 2% inflation, compounding, each year and by their own government, how this erosion is effected by the actions of governments creating money out of thin air, and why, every now and then, a government of the world has a financial crisis with their currency, sometimes affecting all other countries in the world, making it hard for everyday people to make ends meet.

The Fractional Reserve Banking System

For those countries that employ a fractional reserve banking system, basically the government creates money out of thin air when politicians do not have the stomach to raise sufficient revenues by way of taxes for the spending they have promised the populous. Banks get hold of some of that 'money' and are required to hold only a small percentage, a fraction, of that money in reserve while creating more money out of thin air when they effect loans to their customers.

State-Sponsored Fraud?

A simple thought experiment may bring home what the fractional reserve banking system looks like to those who call it *state-sponsored fraud*.

Image the scenario that you go to a meeting with your bank manager to secure a loan. Let us say that the loan is for $10,000.

You sit down with the bank manager, and after polities the bank manager says, *"So how can we help you today?"*

Rather than an expectant course of discourse, you come out with, *"Well, it is like this. I don't have $10,000, but I need it. I know that you do not have $10,000 to lend me, you have anywhere from $0 to $1,000, but I know that the state sponsors your bank to commit fraud and lend to me that which you do not have. So here is what I want you to do; I want you to create $10,000 out of thin air and give that to me on loan. I will not tell anyone that you created the money out of thin air and that it does not really exist. For that privilege, I will repay that loan with interest with real money that I have earned elsewhere."*

Chances are you would not even finish what you were going to say, because you would likely choke at the part where it became obvious to you that the bank expected interest on money they created out of thin air and *loaned* to you, or when it became clear to you that you were somehow becoming complicit in the commission of what would otherwise be considered a crime. If you or I sold something that did not exist, certainly *fraud* is the name for the crime.

It would be an extraordinary scenario, which would likely leave the bank manager flabbergasted and unlikely to give you a *loan*, but that implied conversation effectively happens every day in every country that employs the fractional reserve banking system. Because of decorum or complete ignorance the loaner would never likely say those words and so bluntly. Those words would lift the veil on the effective deceit that is happening when someone secures such a loan.

Extraordinary as it may seem, because all such loans under a fractional reserve banking system are affected in this manner, most of the money in circulation is created by banks. Seed money is created by the *reserve* or *central* bank of the country in a similar arrangement with the government, and *that money* is the source of the *reserves* of other banks. Because of the varied reserve fractions of different banks, it is even the case that many governments of the world have no idea exactly how much money is in circulation, they only have some notion of how much money they initially created and the banks create the rest.

Gold and Precious Metals as Money

While the fractional reserve banking system has permeated most countries on Earth, largely lost to the world is the origin of the system.

Money has historically been a sovereign entity. The ruling government, monarchy or dictatorship of the day had the sovereign right to create, or *mint*, money and declare its use as legal tender throughout whatever realm they governed. For instance, for everyday trade throughout the Roman Empire, people used coins made of gold or silver as money. Gold and silver being metals that are hard to come by made them ideal for money and minting the metals into readily identifiable coins made the money hard to counterfeit because of the technology required to mint the coins. Scarcity is one thing, but another aspect of a precious metal such as gold is that it has utility besides being used for money. This made gold valuable in its own right. For millennia gold has been used to make jewellery to which value and worth is still attributed to this day.

Gold and precious metals not minted as coins were as good as money and anecdotally the story goes that people used to entrust their precious metal with goldsmiths, who made jewellery, for safe keeping [69]. The goldsmith would issue a note (piece of paper) as receipt for the precious metal, and then the note was as good as money for trade, because it could be redeemed for precious metal at the goldsmith. Becoming a form of *paper money* it became obvious to unscrupulous goldsmiths, acting as effective *bankers*, that they could loan out more paper money than they had precious

---

[69] Fractional Reserve Banking, Wikipedia, https://en.wikipedia.org/wiki/Fractional-reserve_banking , Accessed at Saturday, 18 January 2020

metal in reserve. Thus the beginning of banks and fractional reserve lending.

That gold has been used for money is well known, and at one stage the paper money of the United States of America was redeemable for weight in gold, but what is still little known is the divergence of the amount of paper money to actual gold that existed in any similar system. That is, paper money has always been difficult to trust as money, because the extent to which the paper money was devalued by a fractional reserve banking system is largely unknown.

What could possibly go wrong with the fractional reserve banking system?

If paper money ostensibly convertible to gold cannot fully be trusted because the populous cannot be sure there is sufficient gold to back the paper money in circulation, imagine a currency inconvertible to anything!

While a currency can ostensibly be converted to another usable commodity, such as gold, people can at least feel secure that if the ratio from one to the other is reasonably honest then there will not be devaluing of the money by a government creating more money than convertible useable commodity. But if government produced money is not convertible to anything, than a government can produce as much money as its want and devalue the currency considerably. It would be just a matter of time before the populous caught on that there was much more money in circulation than warranted current prices, and the price of goods and services would rise accordingly, *inflation*.

Fiat Money

Regardless of whether the money is paper printed or its electronic equivalent, if it is government minted money inconvertible to anything and in use by government decree, it is called *Fiat Money*.

Gold and precious metal reserves are difficult to inflate aggressively because the metals are difficult to come by. Imagine the government of a country that has its currency backed by gold and where that government wishes to wage war on another country, a very costly exercise. They run the risk of running out of money because they can't find gold fast enough to meet the expenses of the war. Imagine then that the country uses a fiat currency, inconvertible to anything. The government can create as much money as it likes to pay for its war, but at the expense of the currency because overprinting inflates the currency and devalues the currency.

Unless managed very carefully, fiat currencies are particularly onerous for the general populous because governments may not be trusted to not overprint their currency. They may not be waging war, but creating money recklessly to pay for new roads and infrastructure or simply to pay off the government's reckless accumulation of debt. This effectively wages war on the general populous because the inflated currency devalues the spending power of people's hard earned currency. Governments, otherwise entrusted to work for the people, which recklessly inflate their currency effectively enslave the general populous by impoverishing their currency.

History is littered with real world calamities and genuine hardship resulting from governments' hyperinflating a country's currency, but none of that is worth discussing without first looking at inflation itself.

Inflation

As I write this, I sit in a café in North Queensland in Australia, and I have just ordered a cup of coffee that cost me $4.50 in Australian Dollars (AUD). That might not mean much to you if you live in another country using a different currency, but you may be able to relate that 30 years ago that same cup of coffee would have cost me $2.50. It is not that I am at an expensive café, the cost of a cup of coffee is similarly around AUD $5 right across the country, and was around AUD $2 thirty years ago. And it isn't just that the price of coffee has gone up, the cost of living in general has increased similarly in the same timeframe. The relative buying power of the Australian dollar has decreased over time, and the process by which the relative buying power of a unit of currency is deprecated over time is known as inflation; but more pointedly the buying power of the currency is deprecated by the inflation of the amount of money in circulation which depreciates the value of the currency if most other things stay equal.

For instance, if the Australian government, one way or another, inflates the amount of currency in circulation by 2% per annum, but the population of Australia also increases by 2% per annum, it would be hard to imagine that the average cost of goods would have cause to increase because of the inflated money supply. This is because there would be relatively the same amount of money per person in circulation. But if the population did not increase at all, and the money supply increased by 2% the nature of that inflation is that somehow the market becomes aware that there is more money around and prices increase.

Inflation takes on that nature by default when the currency supply is increased disproportionally to the overall size of the economy. Whether by greed or other market force, some suppliers increase their prices. This is noticed by other suppliers that use the goods and services of the first suppliers, and they too increase their prices. They justify their price increases because of the price increases they have experienced. Slowly but surely, if there is lots of money going around, inflation takes hold and the cost of living for the average person increases within the currency that they are using.

The whole process can be exasperated catastrophically if the government creates more and more money in response to their inability to meet their spending habits or loan repayment liabilities. Trying to effectively cheat reality the government prints more money, this becomes evident to the populous or their creditors and prices increase accordingly. This vicious cycle continues until it becomes practically uncontrollable and what is known as *hyperinflation* ensues. Rather than prices steadily growing by 2% per annum, say, prices increase tenfold, 100-fold, 1000-fold, 1 million-fold, 1 billion-fold. The result on the population is devastating. Trust in the currency is effectively reduced to nil, day to day living becomes a race to spend money before it is worthless, and conducting business becomes arduous.

Surprisingly many countries of the word actively target inflation at a rate of approximately 2% per annum. The argument goes that if prices increase and the buying power of a unit of currency decreases, then the populous will be motivated to work harder to earn more money to make up the difference. The problem with this argument is that there is no evidence to say that people would not work hard to earn more money if prices did not increase. When a currency devalues a 2% per annum compounding year after year, within 10 years nearly 20% of the purchasing power of that currency has disappeared. It seems to this author that largely breads distrust in the currency more than motivates people to work harder. The problem with the 'work harder' argument is that if the average wage of people does not increase proportionally to inflation, the general populous loses out anyway. The poor effectively become poorer. Conversely, if wages do increase with inflation one can easily argue, '*why have targeted inflation at all?*'

From all of my research into creation and dissemination of money, the largest complaint that I have heard of when it comes to Fiat currencies is that governments cannot be trusted to resist the temptation to produce more and more currency out of thin air to the detriment of the currency that they inflate and the economy they have the pretext of serving. Many argue that inflation is indirect taxation because the populous is effectively taxed out of their savings by an inflated money supply. While this may be true, even where governments are hesitant to increase direct taxation to meet their want of spending, where that spending is the result of incompetence or corruption, far better to name those things for what they are than fob it off as *indirect taxation.*

When fiat money is combined with a fractional reserve banking system, the problems can compound exponentially.

Before we look at that, let us recap that bitcoin was designed to alleviate the problem of an inflationary money supply, with a total future supply of 21 million bitcoin, and a decreasing inflation rate that halves every four years. This is very noble of the inventor of bitcoin, but which has been largely compromised by the fact that 'bitcoin' has now diverged into multiple bitcoin currencies, of which Bitcoin Cash is only just one currency…effectively inflating the supply of cryptocurrency.

Fiat Money and the Fractional Reserve Banking System

While fiat currencies may be inherently unstable in the long term, the problem is compounded by a fractional reserve banking system. With a fiat currency, the government of the day can inflate the supply of money, but where a fractional reserve banking system is added to the mix…so too can banks inflate the money supply.

If a country has regulations that each bank must have 10%, say, of the money they deal with as deposits, or reserves, the money that they create when making a loan does not just walk out of a bank and not get deposited somewhere. That money too is deposited in a bank, perhaps the same bank, increasing that banks reserves of money. As the basis for creating more money, out of thin air, in subsequent loans, if banks are not careful the money supply could inflate ad infinitum. The only thing keeping that in check is that loans generally come with interest payments required of the debtor and there is only a limited supply of debtors with capacity to meet loan repayments [70].

---

[70] For a lot more information on the fractional reserve banking system head to GoldSilver.com and find their Hidden Secrets of Money section. Similarly on youtube.com at

This has not stopped things getting out of control, and the Global Financial Crisis (GFC) of the year 2008 was effectively the result of escalating credit against an incapacity for that credit to be repaid. Effectively the whole system collapsed in upon itself and extremely large liabilities were written off and banks collapsed. This would not have been so bad if millions of people had not been affected, but because the respective banks made risky loans in order to create more capital, millions of people effectively lost their homes when loans were foreclosed. Largely the result of practices in the United States of America, the financial impacts of the GFC were felt across the globe.

At the time of writing, some twelve years later, the problem of the GFC is still not fully resolved, because rather than allowing for more banks to collapse under the weight of their failed lending practices, the Federal Reserve Bank of the U.S. injected hundreds of billions of dollars, created out of thin air, to bail out the affected banks. While effectively thwarting collapse of more banks, the obvious effect is a sizable inflation of the U.S. money supply.

So what can go wrong with the fractional reserve banking system? A lot can and has gone wrong.

'Credit' – from the Latin 'Credo'

Of course, the word *credit* stems from the Latin, *credo*, which means "to believe'. In Middle French we write *crédit* ("belief, trust"), and in Italian, *credere* is the verb of the same meaning [71].

If we have *good credit* the banks believe in us and our ability to repay debt, but it is ironic that it is our belief in banks which

---

https://www.youtube.com/playlist?list=PLE88E9ICdipidHkTehs1VbFzgwrq1jkUJ

[71] Credit, Wiktionary, https://en.wiktionary.org/wiki/credit, Accessed at Tuesday, 21 January 2020

gives banks power to judge our credit in the first place.

Banks deal in credit and one of the biggest complaints about the fractional reserve banking system that I have encountered in researching this book is that banks effectively create money out of thin air when they create credit on their ledgers with each loan they create. This complaint is largely justified when we look at the problems that it creates, but I feel the complaint misses a key point. That is that money has to come from somewhere, and if there is not enough gold and precious metal to serve the size of an economy then an economy would always be stifled by limited supply. This is true regardless of unscrupulous banks or governments. So credit is responsible for a large proportion of money in existence and reduces to belief in people, a deceitful system and fiat money itself.

Credit, or belief and trust, is ultimately at the core of money whether it is fiat money or otherwise. We believe in currencies of limited supply because we do not trust that a government or a bank will not inflate our money away, and we believe in a fiat currency until such time as we no longer trust in the currency at all because it has been inflated away. Originally trust in a debtor rather than a physical or conceptual thing such as money, credit has evolved into a belief system where all of money is largely given value by the belief people hold that it holds a certain value.

For example, when there were no people on the Earth, the gold metal element still existed, but there were no people to give any value to gold. It is people that give gold value. The same is true of paper money, electronic money and a currency such as Bitcoin Cash. Money is what we collectively say it is and its value is what we collectively give it.

Money vs. Currency

If you search the internet for the difference between money and currency, you are likely to find many conflicting definitions.

One of the most useful distinctions that I have found is that commodities such as gold and silver may be thought of as *money*, given that they are real and tangible goods, and where as a *currency* is better represented by what we generally trade with today, paper money and its electronic counterpart. This position, however, is largely supported by those who trade in gold and silver and have a vested interest in considering those commodities as *real money*. Their argument, is that because gold and silver have historically (with exceptions) held value over time and have been used as money from time immemorial, that gold and silver are 'real money', whereas all fiat currencies are merely currencies. In everyday vernacular, however, I have never encountered anyone making a big deal out of calling cash *money*, indeed everyone I know does.

To this extent, I feel that it is pointless trying to distinguish between money and currency, as to the layperson both terms are used in such an inter-dispersed manner that the line is too blurred for it to be meaningful to people.

Is Bitcoin Money or Currency?

So what is Bitcoin? Is it money or currency? As discussed in the open chapters of this book, in your country the government may consider it neither for tax reason or when considering Bitcoin as any form of legal tender. Given the name, cryptocurrency, there will be those who call Bitcoin a currency. If you look at the bitcoincash.org website, Bitcoin Cash is "Sound money for the world". In the next chapter we look at this claim in detail.

Bitcoin Cash - "Sound Money to the World"

In August 2017, Bitcoin Cash was born as a currency separate from Bitcoin Core. Proponents set up a website, www.bitcoincash.org, to help promote Bitcoin Cash and invite people to start using the currency. The site also invites software developers and miners to move to Bitcoin Cash and what the currency stands for through the eyes of the currency creators.

The proponents of Bitcoin Cash who maintain Bitcoincash.org write that "Bitcoin Cash brings sound money to the world" without extrapolating on what *sound money* actually is. We are left to our own devices to form our own opinion by other writing on the website. Of course, the idea of money that is sound does *sound* attractive, so let us look at that carefully.

The adjective, sound, has multiple meanings, all of which inflect a positive quality [72]:

financially secure and safe – "a sound investment", "a sound economy"

healthy, exercising good judgment – "sound judgement", "sound advice"

in good condition, free from defect – "a sound foundation"

reasoned, well-grounded – "a sound argument"

free from moral defect – "a person of sound character"

---

[72] Largely adapted from the definitions found in WordNet, an initiative of the Princeton University. See http://wordnetweb.princeton.edu/perl/webwn?s=sound&sub=Search+WordNet v, Accessed at Tuesday, 28 January 2020

profound, heavy, deep and complete – "a sound sleep"

thorough – "a sound thrashing"

It is likely that proponents of Bitcoin Cash mean a combination of all of those qualities when they speak of Bitcoin Cash and bitcoin in general. Indeed, Satoshi Nakamoto made what has come to be seen as a political statement within the very first information stored within the bitcoin database when bitcoin was first released in 2009, hinting that she was creating a more sound money. Known as the Genesis Block, the first information in the bitcoin database contains the words,

"The Times 03/Jan/2009 Chancellor on brink of second bailout for banks"

This is the headlines from The Times newspaper of the United Kingdom from the 3rd January 2009, which both cements in time the commencement of the bitcoin network and seems to make the political statement that bitcoin is here to challenge existing currency systems that see governments bailing out banks by forgiving their misguided lending practices by creating even more inflationary currency out of thin air to effect those bailouts.

Nine years after the advent of Bitcoin the Governor of the Bank of England in his speech on The Future of Money, put it this way…"[I]n the depths of the global financial crisis, the coincidence of technological developments and collapsing confidence in some banking systems sparked the cryptocurrency revolution." [73]

---

[73] Speech by Dr Mark Carney, Governor of the Bank of England, The Future of Money, 2 March 2018, https://www.bankofengland.co.uk/speech/2018/mark-carney-speech-to-the-inaugural-scottish-economics-conference, Accessed at Tuesday, 5 November 2018

It is clear that Nakamoto felt that she was releasing sound money to the world, but what makes bitcoin sound money, and what makes bitcoin cash sound money?

Part of what differentiated bitcoin from fiat currency became apparent from the start. The total future supply of bitcoin would be limited to 21 million bitcoin. The idea being to bring currency back to where supply is limited.

When Bitcoin Cash separated from Bitcoin Core the creators did something extraordinary however, they kept the ledger of Bitcoin the same up until the cutover to Bitcoin Cash and effectively copied that ledger over to Bitcoin Cash. So everyone who held Bitcoin Core now held the same amount of Bitcoin Cash. This effectively doubled the supply of bitcoin. Different exchange rates for each currency challenge this proposal, the size of the economy did not double, but the premise of inflation was introduced to bitcoin and not long after the release of bitcoin cash the exchange rate for bitcoin core collapsed significantly. The notion of *sound money* was challenged almost immediately.

For the purposes of this book we look closer at what drove people to break away from Bitcoin Core, in the next chapter. Here we presume that proponents of Bitcoin Cash aim to leave Bitcoin Core in the dust and for the exchange rate of Bitcoin Core to continue to decline as Bitcoin Cash increases in strength…becoming the dominant bitcoin. Similarly, if Nakamoto's was a political statement then Nakamoto seems to have set out to rid the world of currency that is otherwise unsound, and create a currency that is sound, bitcoin.

Through that lens we can look at Bitcoin Cash and what is seen to make *that* a sound currency.

If we explore the dictionary properties of soundness already proffered in relation to Bitcoin Cash, we get the following:

Soundness Qualities   **Sound Qualities of Bitcoin Cash**

Secure and Safe	In 1933 the US government forced its citizens to surrender the gold that was stored in their homes to help prop-up the currency of the United States.

Bitcoin Cash cannot easily be confiscated as it is possible to create effective accounts that nobody knows about except those who own the accounts.

Bitcoin Cash, as an electronic money network, is particularly difficult and on the whole impossible to defraud if you know what you are doing. The network itself is relatively secure and safe, but you should read the chapter, Problems with Bitcoin Cash, to gauge that security. |
| **Exercising Good Judgement** | Money, as inanimate, does not exercise and judgement, but this aspect of key people who promote Bitcoin Cash is highly debatable. See the chapter, Problems with Bitcoin Cash, for more information. |
| **Free from defect** | Bitcoin has a good reputation as being a very secure electronic money network, but serious bugs have been found in the Bitcoin Cash source code in the past.

It is a function of the people behind maintaining Bitcoin Cash that will determine whether Bitcoin Cash remains |

free from defect. The thesis of this book is that you are required to trust that the people managing the bitcoin cash network know what they are doing in order to trust Bitcoin Cash.

Reasoned, well-grounded	There are serious questions as to whether key people who promote the Bitcoin Cash ecosystem are reasoned or well-grounded in their approach. We look at the commonly regarded qualities of sound money separate from people, next.
	See the chapter, Problems with Bitcoin Cash, for more information.
Free from moral defect	Money, as inanimate, has no morals to speak of, but we can question the key people who promote Bitcoin Cash as to whether they are free of moral defect.
	See the chapter, Problems with Bitcoin Cash, for more information.
Profound, heavy, deep and complete	A lot of thought went into the original release of bitcoin. Nakamoto obviously thought seriously about the qualities of sound money. We look at that next. In as much as proponents of Bitcoin Cash aim to extend the vision of Nakamoto it could be claimed that Bitcoin Cash is profound, heavy, deep and complete.
Thoroughly thought through	In that Bitcoin Cash is a working electronic cash network processing significant amounts of electronic cash transactions per day, it is hard to argue that Bitcoin Cash is not thoroughly

thought through.

There are serious questions as to whether those who promote Bitcoin Cash, however, have thoroughly thought through their actions. See the chapter, Problems with Bitcoin Cash, for more information.

So if we take the dictionary meaning of soundness we focus more on qualities imbued by people themselves rather than qualities of an inanimate concept such as money. The thesis of this book is that it is inescapable that the people in charge of maintaining the Bitcoin Cash network must be considered as much as the qualities of the currency itself.

As to whether Bitcoin Cash is sound money separate from human qualities, we are in luck. Economists and those who study money have come up with a list of qualities that the money must possess in order to be sound money. Let us look at these.

Quality of Money	Qualities of Bitcoin Cash
Scarcity	Bitcoin Cash is limited to 21million BCH, with some 18,200,000 BCH in circulation at early 2020. Nakamoto even quipped: "Lost coins only make everyone else's coins worth slightly more. Think of it as a donation to everyone." [74] **NB** See the next section of this book "Bitcoin as a Store of Value" for more information

---

[74] Lost bitcoin, Bitcointalk.org, https://bitcointalk.org/index.php?topic=198.msg1647#msg1647 , Accessed at Wednesday, 22 January 2020

about the inflationary effect of splitting from Bitcoin Core. Another issue for Bitcoin Cash is that it is only one of more than 5000 cryptocurrencies in existence. Bitcoin Cash may be scarce but cryptocurrency is not scarce.

Durability   Each Bitcoin Cash will last as long as the network is kept alive by those who operate the network, which will ultimately be determined by the profitability of those who operate the network.

NB See the section "Mining Bitcoin Cash" for more information on the profitability of mining Bitcoin Cash and maintaining the network.

Portability   As a digital asset Bitcoin Cash is extremely portable. While the real value of Bitcoin Cash is within the network spanning the globe, a Bitcoin Cash wallet used to access value stored on the network easily runs on a smartphone and can be taken anywhere a person travels with their smartphone.

NB Of course, access to the internet is required to use a wallet to transfer Bitcoin Cash to another wallet.

Divisibility   Each Bitcoin Cash is divisible by 100 million parts, each called a satoshi.

Fungibility   All Bitcoin Cash are considered equal.

Storable   Bitcoin Cash is stored within the global and distributed database that forms the backbone of the network (the Bitcoin Cash blockchain).

The size of this database will grow over time, and limit the number of people with capacity to store the database; however this may not be problematic with storage capacity increasing over the same time, and cost of storage capacity decreasing over the same time.

Difficult to Counterfeit

By default of the design of the software of Bitcoin Cash, and with the technology of the foreseeable future, it is regarded as almost impossible to counterfeit Bitcoin Cash. The network actively protects against double-spending of Bitcoin Cash which is the closest correlation there is between copying of the digital currency and counterfeiting of paper/coin based money.

NB It seems that a double spend on the Bitcoin Core network has happened at least once before the problem was corrected [75]

Widely used and accepted

There are thousands of locations across the world where Bitcoin Cash can be spent. The Marco Coino app for smartphones shows where Bitcoin Cash can be spent.

Easily Transferrable / Convenient

It is very easy to transfer Bitcoin Cash from one wallet to another. The receiving party/wallet does not need to be connected to the internet to receive Bitcoin Cash.

Stability as a measure of value / unit of

At the time of writing this (early 2020) bitcoin is rarely used as a measure of value. I have witnessed no good or service priced in Bitcoin

---

[75] Double spending of Bitcoin, bitcointalk.org, https://bitcointalk.org/index.php?topic=152348, Accessed at Wednesday, 22 January 2020

account	Cash.

In relation to other currencies, for example the U.S. dollar, Bitcoin Cash has historically been quite volatile. Launching in the vicinity of U.S. $1200 per Bitcoin Cash, BCH trades at about U.S. $349 in early 2020, recovering from a low of approximately U.S. $80 in late 2018. The entire year of 2019 saw steady gains for BCH against the U.S. dollar.

Stability - general

In regards to an electronic monetary network it is safe to say that Bitcoin Cash is relatively stable, with nearly 100% up-time and no system outages to speak of. This is remarkable for an electronic monetary system.

The regulatory framework for Bitcoin Cash is stable in some countries and unsure in others.

Store of Value

If you bought one Bitcoin Cash for over U.S. $2500 in early 2018 you would not consider Bitcoin Cash a particularly good store of value with the exchange price at U.S. $349 in early 2020, but if you bought at U.S. $80 in late 2018 you would.

What is remarkable about Bitcoin Cash is that compared to the thousands of other cryptocurrencies created since the advent of bitcoin, Bitcoin Cash seems to be maintaining and gaining ground. Many cryptocurrencies simply disappear through lack of support, but having followed the number of places accepting Bitcoin Cash (on the Marco Coino app for smartphones) over the last year while researching this book, I can safely say that the Bitcoin Cash ecosystem is growing.

The number of transactions per day on the network, visible to anyone, has however remained static over the last year. This is positive in respect that it is not going down.

This static persistence of Bitcoin Cash lends to the notion that Bitcoin Cash is somewhat credible as a store of value.

Non-repudiable   If the network reflects that Bitcoin Cash has been received by the recipient, there is no question that they did receive the bitcoin. This is particularly true the longer the transaction is recorded on the network.

Transparency   The total number of Bitcoin Cash in circulation at any one time is publically available information.

Because the Bitcoin Cash transaction database is distributed to every computer running the Bitcoin Cash software and connected to the network, a wide range of information is publically accessible about Bitcoin Cash. This includes the number of transactions per day, the average and mean value of transactions, the number of unique addresses (wallets effectively) using the network. Contrasted to a traditional fiat currency this is extraordinary information to have readily available.

Recognizable   The name *bitcoin* is recognisable across the world at this stage, but with varying degree of understanding about the currency. It is undoubtedly confusing that there is more than one bitcoin.

Bitcoin as a Store of Value

One of the most interesting uses of Bitcoin is as a store of value. If you bought Bitcoin in 2011 at U.S. $1 and held onto that Bitcoin until 2018, the value of your Bitcoin would be worth USD$6400, and your equivalent amount of Bitcoin Cash would be worth USD$430. That is not just holding value; that is vastly appreciating in value.

Increased awareness and a bullish prediction on the future relevance of Bitcoin has almost certainly driven market demand, but deep within the psychology of Bitcoin holders is the notion that Bitcoin should increase in value over time given that the future supply is limited to 21million Bitcoin.

If a currency needs belief in order to exist as a currency, then the central belief that bitcoin should hold and increase in value over time is one belief that may sustain bitcoin over time.

Given that there are now many variants of bitcoin, however, this central belief will be equally tested over time because the deflationary quality of one variant of bitcoin is only characteristic to that variant in isolation. If people keep creating new bitcoin variants on a whim, the cryptocurrency ecosystem as a whole becomes inflationary.

Bitcoin is inflationary

There is a general misconception that bitcoin is inherently deflationary, because the total supply of bitcoin will be limited. While true of the future bitcoin is currently inflationary and will be until the year 2140.

Nakamoto wrote in the initial email announcing the release of bitcoin [76]:

---

[76] Satoshi Nakamoto releases bitcoin, The Mail Archive, https://www.mail-

```
Total circulation will be 21,000,000 coins.
It'll be distributed to network nodes when they
make blocks, with the amount cut in half every 4
years.

first 4 years: 10,500,000 coins
next 4 years: 5,250,000 coins
next 4 years: 2,625,000 coins
next 4 years: 1,312,500 coins > etc...
```

In early 2020 the Bitcoin Cash inflation rate is approximately 3.8%, a value that is widely seen by economists to be high for a currency and detrimental to an economy. But in about May 2020 the inflation rate will drop to around 1.9% which will place Bitcoin Cash as a currency with an inflation rate less than the targeted 2% inflation of many Western countries.

Bitcoin Reward Halving

The way that the Bitcoin Cash software is designed, every four years the number of new Bitcoin Cash issued by the network every ten minutes is halved. In January 2020 there were 12.5 bitcoin cash issued approximately every 10 minutes.

It is theorised that because of Bitcoin reward halving, and that the supply of Bitcoin is reduced by such throttling, that the value of Bitcoin will increase as a result of each halving event. The Bitcoin Cash network is relatively young, but empirical evidence on the Bitcoin Core network shows that Bitcoin has indeed increased in value over time spans that range over a Bitcoin reward halving events.

The result of Bitcoin reward halving is that in the year 2140 there will be the last reward halving as the reward awarded to a successful miner each 10 minutes will be zero and for which halving of zero is zero. The ultimate result of this process is that

archive.com/cryptography@metzdowd.com/msg10152.html, Accessed at Friday, 24 January 2020 there will never be more than approximately 21 million Bitcoin Cash ever produced. It is this relative scarcity of Bitcoin Cash that may lead to Bitcoin Cash being an effective store of value over time. But that value will only be achieved if Bitcoin Cash is in demand.

As an event worth tracking, some websites have set up Bitcoin Cash countdown timers. One such countdown timer can be found at: https://coinsalad.com/bitcoincash/halving

The Bitcoin Reward Halving Conundrum

If Bitcoin continues to appreciate in value relative to fiat currencies because of bitcoin reward halving an interesting conundrum ensues; if someone spends their bitcoin and is not earning an income in bitcoin, then it will cost that person more in fiat currency to replace the bitcoin they have spent to further appreciate bitcoin as a store of value.

This conundrum has arguably lead to people holding onto their bitcoin, in the absence of a bitcoin economy where people earn money as bitcoin and where merchants set prices for goods in bitcoin, in the hope that bitcoin will increase in price relative to fiat currency. This type of speculative is known within the bitcoin vernacular as a HODLer or someone who "Holds On for Dear Life" to their bitcoin.

HODLer Mentality

Paradoxically, if every user of bitcoin as a currency holds on to their bitcoin for dear life, in the hope of selling that bitcoin for fiat currency and at a profit, then bitcoin would never become a useful currency, because nobody would be spending their bitcoin.

If nobody spends their bitcoin, then it may be argued that there will be less demand for bitcoin (other than for HODLer purposes). If the demand for bitcoin becomes low then why would the market price of bitcoin increase at all?

In this respect, the HODLer mentality may be seen as detrimental to bitcoin as a whole and result in bitcoin becoming ineffective as a currency for regular trading of goods and services.

If a merchant sets prices in bitcoin, and the price of bitcoin increases relative to the fiat currency a person is earning, then those goods will become unattractive. Whereas if people earn their income in bitcoin, and where because of the eventual deflationary quality of bitcoin, the relative price of goods fall in value, this will make it attractive for people to both hold bitcoin and purchase items with bitcoin. We discuss deflation later in this book.

Either way you look at it, bitcoin as a store of value is only interesting if countries continue to have fiat currencies under which people are paid, and where bitcoin increases in price relative to those fiat currencies, or if everyone is paid in bitcoin and goods prices are set in bitcoin making the price of goods relative to earnings fall in price by the eventual deflation of bitcoin.

Bitcoin Cash vs. Bitcoin Core

The market dynamic which would see a currency which is not readily spent diminish in value through lack of demand, is one of the primary reasons Bitcoin Cash was formed to break away from Bitcoin Core. With refusal to scale Bitcoin Core, the transaction fees for Bitcoin Core reached U.S. $50 per transaction in late 2017. Subsequently the exchange price of Bitcoin Core fell from around U.S. $20,000 per coin to U.S $3,000 per coin as the market became disillusioned with Bitcoin Core. Bitcoin Cash, conversely, consistently maintains transaction fees at less than U.S. 1cent.

The network gives value to Bitcoin Cash

We explored the value proposition of Bitcoin Cash in the chapter, "What is Money?", but here we suffice ourselves with the knowledge that it is the extent, robustness and utility of the Bitcoin Cash network that ultimately gives Bitcoin Cash value.

The overall extent of the Bitcoin Cash network is best quantitatively measured by the number of full mining nodes that actively validate transactions in order to receive Bitcoin cash rewards (as Bitcoin Cash). As at October 2018 a curated count of the active full mining nodes running the Bitcoin Cash network puts the number of nodes at 1887 nodes (https://cash.coin.dance/nodes). This means that there are at least 1887 computers around the world running the Bitcoin Cash network. Each full mining node, however, employs anything from 1 to many hundreds (to thousands) of other computers to assist the mining node in the task of strengthening and effectively running the Bitcoin Cash network. While these nodes continue to operate profitably, it is safe to say that the Bitcoin Cash network will continue to operate.

The extent of the Bitcoin Cash network is what also makes the Bitcoin Cash network robust. The more nodes supporting a network the harder it is for the network to collapse or be shut down.

An extensive and robust network of computers, however, will not drive demand for a product or service, there needs to be more. For the vision of Bitcoin Cash to be 'sound money for the world' to be realised, there must be sufficient utility of the currency for people to want to use it.

What will drive Bitcoin Cash Demand?

A currency is useless unless people are actually using that currency for some purpose. It is a natural question to ask what will drive demand for Bitcoin Cash such that it is used for some profitable purpose by people.

The answer to that question is varied and will depend on many factors going forward.

A primary use case is needed – Store of Value is not enough

We have already seen that the Store of Value quality of Bitcoin is already a recognised use of Bitcoin. Historically and depending on when someone acquired Bitcoin, this use case has variably led to riches or ruin. For Store of Value to be a viable use of Bitcoin Cash over time, it seems clear that store of value must be a secondary use case if Bitcoin Cash is to be sound money. Why?

Unlike a commodity such as gold, bitcoin only really has value if the computer network that supports that bitcoin is running. If all the computers running the Bitcoin Cash network were to shut down, the Bitcoin Cash stored in the ledger would be worthless. The miners are only motivated to continue running the Bitcoin Cash network if they make a profit. They will only make a profit if the value of the Bitcoin Cash they earn from maintaining the network is enough to cover their expenses, or similarly the value of the transaction fees they earn for the transactions processed on the network. With the amount of Bitcoin Cash earned by mining reduced by 50% each four years, then if the value of each Bitcoin does not double each four years, then the amount of money earned from fees must increase in order to meet costs. Simply increasing fees drives customers away, as seen on the Bitcoin Core network, so the number of transactions must increase to meet the shortfall.

The primary reason for Bitcoin Cash's existence stems from the belief of the developers of Bitcoin Cash that Store of Value alone is not a sufficiently attractive use of Bitcoin such that the currency would actually drive demand for Bitcoin to be an effective store of value in the first place. Low cost transaction fees, and lots of transactions, must attract people to use and maintain the network.

In terms of sound money, rarity by itself does not of itself make something valuable. The reasons for this become obvious if we look at whether or not works of art are an effective store of value. Historically, works of art are an effective store of value *if* they are rare and desirable. I could, however, paint a one-off picture that would be of no marketable value. I might succeed in my endeavours, but I would stand more chance of success if my work of art was at least beautiful or interesting to behold. I would be giving my work a viable use case. Bitcoin Cash proponents argue that Bitcoin Core's primary use case, a store of value, falls flat in a market economy that demands low fees and where miners require a profit to be made to uphold the bitcoin network.

Bitcoin Cash proponents argue that by providing utility in providing a low cost value transfer (payment) network designed to scale to millions of transactions per day, this design will provide Bitcoin Cash a competitive edge over the Bitcoin Core network. This is how they aim to achieve what they perceive as sound money. Relying solely on a *store of value* premise would lead to a simply speculative market, and no currency use. A Ponzi scheme if you will.

The Greater Fool Theory

Detractors of Bitcoin say that because Bitcoin is backed by nothing (e.g. gold) that it has no intrinsic value. At first glance, that seems to make sense. That is until you realise that fiat currencies are backed by nothing.

The Greater Fool Theory maintains that people buy an asset of some description in the hope and expectation that it will go up in price and that they will be able to sell that asset to an even greater fool who purchases the asset for the same reason.

The Greater Fool Theory makes perfect sense when you think about Bitcoin, until you realise that when you trade effort for fiat currency, in the hope and expectation that the money you hold will hold its value until someone else effectively buys that money from you through their efforts when they sell you some good or service. What is extraordinary about the fiat currencies issued by most governments of the world, is that you sell your money to other people in the full knowledge that, if kept in their hands as savings, that money will actually depreciate by 2% annually (or depreciate by close to 20% in 10 years!). This happens, of course, by inflation. So who is the bigger fool? Someone who trades in a currency designed to have ever decreasing inflation over time, Bitcoin, or someone trading in a currency where governments (through their reserve banks) actively inflate away value at a targeted 2% each year?

It makes for an interesting thought, and Gavin Andresen says in SQ1.tv's documentary "The Bitcoin Phenomenon", that the world's economists will need to rethink economics, based on the fact that Bitcoin (BTC) had become the most expensive currency in the world [77].

Where Bitcoin Cash aims to at least justify the value of bitcoin is by having a network that is widely used for everyday type expenses, and store of value as a secondary use case.

---

[77] "The Bitcoin Phenomenon", SQ1.tv, https://www.youtube.com/watch?v=6pWblf8COH4, Accessed at Wednesday. 29 January 2020

The Great Scaling Debate

What I find intriguing about cryptocurrencies such as Bitcoin Cash is that the respective community airs its dirty linen in public and effectively turns the electronic banking industry inside out. Most banking solutions keep as many secrets as they can, but things are very public in a cryptocurrency world.

For example, have you any idea of what internal debates rage over technology, economics and personnel inside a traditional bank? Are you any the wiser as to whom is the lead software developer or solution architect of the IT infrastructure of a traditional bank?

The answer is most likely, *no*. Such things are private in traditional banks, and probably for good reason. You do not want to be concerned about how your grocery purchase payment goes through cheaply, reliably and efficiently, just that it does. If you use Visa or MasterCard at a shop to buy something via an electronic payment, you do not know or care about the thousands of hours of hard work that have gone into making that transaction as seamless and effortless as possible. You just swipe or wave your card, and voila, your payment is done.

Indeed, if the software developers of traditional banking payments went public with the issues of whether or not the banking infrastructure could handle the volume of transactions being processed, they would likely have their employment terminated; especially if the debate pointed fingers at other people and technologies, and upset important people.

Traditional marketing to promote confidence in the electronic banking system seems to rely on selling the final product, seamless and effortless transactions. The only time you care whether or not the electronic banking system works is when it does not and you are left at the checkout of your supermarket with no way of paying for your goods. It happens rarely, but I have seen it happen when I worked at a supermarket.

Debates over technology driving a cryptocurrency, on the other hand, are often public affairs. Passionate and often vicious at the same time, proponents air their views in public forums such as www.twitter.com and www.reddit.com. Bitcoin is no exception and has had long running debates aired in the open over many years.

One such debate is "The Great Scaling Debate" over whether Bitcoin software should be designed to handle large volumes of transactions in a short period of time.

You would think that such a question would be trivially resolved. If the bitcoin network was ever to compete against payment networks like Visa or MasterCard, bitcoin would at least have to be able to handle the same level of transaction traffic as those networks. It is hard to pinpoint when the debate started in earnest, some say as early as 2011, but we now know that the scaling debate has been settled, with Bitcoin Cash breaking away from Bitcoin Core on 1st August 2017 to become its own cryptocurrency and where Bitcoin Cash is designed to handle millions of transactions per day.

To understand why exponents of Bitcoin Cash felt they had to break away from Bitcoin Core to settle the debate, we need to know more about Satoshi Nakamoto's invention. We need to know more about the details of how Bitcoin works. This is probably the least attractive thing to a consumer, however, as it is hardly necessary to know how an engine works in order to drive a car; but it is necessary to understand the genius behind Nakamoto's invention if we are ever to understand Bitcoin Cash. Let us look under the hood.

Nakamoto's Invention of Bitcoin

Nakamoto's white paper outlining the machinations of Bitcoin provided a solution to a problem that had plagued earlier attempts at developing electronic cash.

The central problem with electronic cash is that electronic data is very easy to copy and duplicate. If I have a photo stored as a digital file, a .jpg file for instance, it is very easy for me to make copies of that file and send it to all my friends. What if I had an electronic representation of a coin? I could easily make copies of that coin and send it to multiple people, effectively spending the same coin twice, three times, infinitely many times. This problem is known as the *double-spending problem*.

Nakamoto's invention of Bitcoin provided a solution to the double-spending problem by implementing a globally distributed ledger of transactions and where consensus as to the state of that ledger is achieved by a proof-of-work.

That sounds all very complicated, but is easy to understand when it is broken down into its component parts.

It is easy to imagine a digital cash system having a record of coins and a mechanism by which owners of those coins claim ownership of those coins. If you bundle all of those coins into an effective ledger of all the available coins, all the better; each of the coins can be stored in a ledger stored in a database. The problem that existed for previous attempts at digital cash was that a central authority of some description (e.g. a company) maintained the ledger as a single database and where that same authority was responsible for identifying and eliminating double-spends. Such arrangements were very easy to shut down; shut down the company and the central database and you have shut down the whole digital cash system. Why shut down a digital cash system? Well governments prefer to have the sovereign right to mint money and control monetary systems. Digital cash systems, such a bitcoin, are run extraneously to governments.

So Nakamoto devised a system where multiple copies of the ledger, as a database, exists around the globe and where collectively the group of globally distributed software running a copy of the bitcoin software decides over which transactions are valid, and which were attempts at a double-spend. For example, Bitcoin Cash has over 1000 copies of its ledger distributed around the world and over 1000 computers validating the ledger.

But how do people, or the software in this case, around the world agree on which transaction is valid, and which a double-spend, if each does not necessarily trust any of the other players in the system? Which transactions do you trust, and how do you know that your copy of the database is the same as everyone else's copy of the database? Even if the players all trust each other, which version of events do you trust to put in your copy of the database?

Nakamoto's solution to this problem is what ultimately has become known as a work of genius. It is a solution to what is known as the Byzantine Generals' Problem, which itself is worth examining to make it easier to understand how Bitcoin works under the hood [78].

The Byzantine Generals Problem was hypothesised by a group of computer scientists in 1982, and is characterised like this [79]:

1. Several divisions of the Byzantine army are camped outside an enemy city, each division commanded by its own general;

---

[78] Nakamoto tries to explain the Byzantine Generals Problem, www.metzdowd.com, https://www.metzdowd.com/pipermail/cryptography/2008-November/014849.html , Accessed at Monday, 27 January 2020

[79] Lamport, L.; Shostak, R.; Pease, M. (1982), "The Byzantine Generals Problem", ACM Transactions on Programming Languages and Systems

2. The generals can communicate with one another only by messenger;

3. After observing the enemy, they must collectively decide upon a common plan of action...to attack or retreat;

4. Some of the generals may be traitors, trying to prevent the loyal generals from reaching agreement;

5. The generals must have an strategy to guarantee that all loyal generals decide upon the same plan of action and a small number of traitors cannot cause the loyal generals to adopt a bad plan;

6. The loyal generals will all do what the strategy says they should, but the traitors may do anything they wish; and

7. The loyal generals should not only reach agreement, but should agree upon a reasonable plan, regardless of what the traitors do.

The problem is twofold. Which of the generals makes the decision that the others must follow? And, no general can be in complete trust of all the other generals.

It is a difficult problem to solve, but is exactly the problem Nakamoto needed to solve in order to make Bitcoin a reality. Every instance of the Bitcoin software represents a general, and the decision over whether a transaction is a double-spend or not is the decision of a general as to whether to attack or not.

Let us call each instance of the Bitcoin software running on a computer a *node,* as for the convention of nodes running in a peer-to-peer software network. The ultimate problem for Bitcoin is for each node to decide which version of the ledger, which each of them maintains, is the valid ledger. Of course, if each node has to have the same ledger for the ledger to make any economic sense, and so each node must communicate with other nodes to share transactions that it has processed so that each node is kept up to date.

Nakamoto's solution to the problem was to have each node lump a set of transactions that the node has validated to not be double-spends into what she called a *block* of transactions. On receiving any transaction from another node and where that transaction had not been seen before by the first node, the first node would transmit the transaction to other nodes that it was connected to. Individual nodes are not connected to all other nodes, but because each node is connected to various nodes a network is formed.

The node would at the same time try and solve a simple-to-define but long-to-execute maths problem and when the problem had been solved, the node races to transmit the block of transaction information that it has prepared to all the nodes that it is connected to, and they in turn pass the block onto other nodes. The process of solving the maths problem is known as a *Proof of Work*.

On receiving the block of transactions from another node in the network, each node would both validate that there were no double-spends within the transactions in the block and that the sending node had genuinely performed the Proof of Work.

Checking to see that there is no double-spends within the block is easy, each node has a copy of the ledger, so they can check that a coin within the ledger had not been spent before. But how does each node know that the node that sent the block had actually performed the Proof of Work?

That much, it turns out, is pretty easy. The *proof* of the Proof of Work is the output of the maths problem itself. Basically that output corresponds to a number, or value, that could only have been calculated if its inputs were the previous proof of work output and a lot of computational power operating over that previous value to come up with the new value. The node sending the *new* block must have had the *previous* block, which in turn must have been produced with knowledge and work over the previous block before that...all the way back to the very first block of transactions. The output of the proof of work is added to the block of transactions in what is known as a *header*, and where each block header demonstrates that a proof of work has been performed over the block before that and all subsequent new transactions. This chain of blocks has come to be known as a *blockchain* [80].

Conceptually, the blockchain looks like the image below:

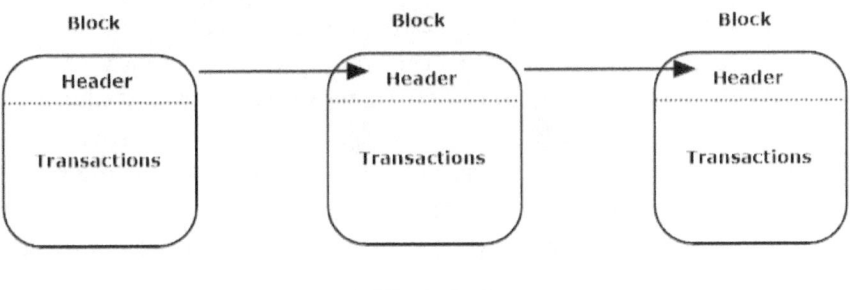

A Blockchain

It turns out that if each node accepts each new block fashioned in this way, and where the block contains no double-spends and has a correct header Proof of Work, then if better than half of the nodes in the network are honest (i.e. not trying to defraud the system), then it is practically impossible for a malicious node to defraud the system.

Tracking back to the Byzantine Generals Problem, each node now has its algorithm, or strategy, to work with, and each general following this strategy has a way to reach consensus over whether to attack or retreat, or in our case, whether to accept transactions into the block-chain or not.

---

[80] For technocrats, the transactions of a block are hashed into header, https://bitcointalk.org/index.php?action=profile;u=3;sa=showPosts;start=42 0, and each header is hashed into the chain, effectively tying the transactions to the header and block chain.

You might ask, *but what if all the nodes/generals are dishonest or traitors?* In this case the whole system falls down. But Nakamoto found a way to motivate the operators of nodes to be honest, by rewarding them in bitcoin if they were honest.

The Proof of Work algorithm is designed such that no single node can dominate the proceedings because the chance of finding the next proof of work is quasi-random, and each node in the network is in a race to find the next proof of work based on their computer processing power. The Proof of Work algorithm is also throttled, becoming harder or easier depending on how quickly the problem is being solved. This throttling keeps blocks flowing at a rate of approximately 1 block every 10 minutes. We have already seen in an earlier chapter, that each node is incentivised to maintain the block-chain and check for no double-spends by being issued new bitcoin. This new bitcoin is given to the node that solves the Proof of Work. Nodes that run the software checking the Proof of Work in order to receive the reward became known as *mining nodes*, as if mining for new bitcoin.

This consensus protocol has come to be known as *Nakamoto Consensus* and is the key invention of Bitcoin.

How does each mining node know which ledger is valid? Well, each node keeps a copy of the ledger, made up of blocks. The scheme is known as an *Open Distributed Ledger*.

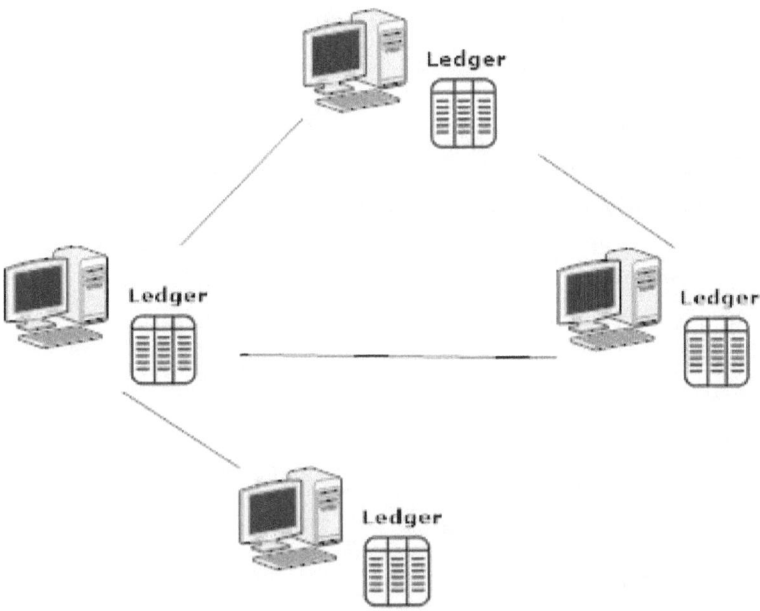

An Open Distributed Ledger

NB People do try and double-spend on the Bitcoin Cash network, but one or the other of the transactions does not make it onto the ledger. A site tracks those attempts: https://doublespend.cash/ . Once a transaction is sufficiently deep within the blockchain, say 6 blocks deep, it can be considered part of the consensus ledger.

The Forked Block-Chain

There are minutiae within the Bitcoin protocol that are pivotal to how Bitcoin works, but which became key to the birth of Bitcoin Cash.

What happens if two nodes solve the Proof of Work at the same time, or when a subsequent node receives two blocks at the same time? Bitcoin's answer is that the node holds both nodes as candidates to add to the block-chain until the next subsequent block is found adding to one of two deadlocked blocks, breaking the deadlock. The losing block is discarded and the problem is naturally resolved.

This strategy works perfectly in practice, but raises the question: *"What if some of the nodes followed a different set of consensus rules than the other nodes in the network?"*

The answer there is that the blockchain would split into two blockchains and effectively become a *forked blockchain*, as below:

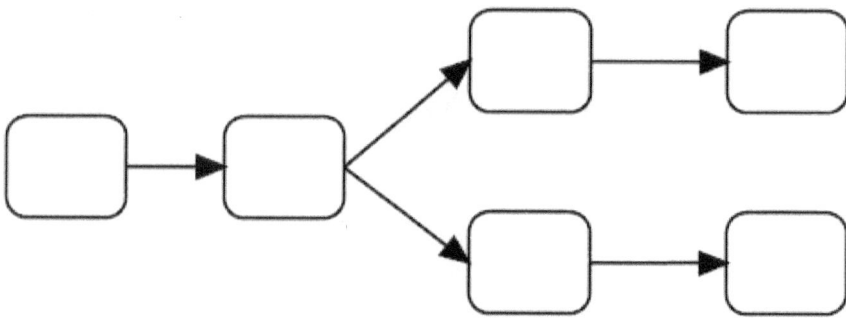

A Forked Blockchain

In practice, this will only happen by accident if some nodes ran software that contained bugs, or deliberately if some nodes ran versions of the software with intentional changes to the consensus rules.

NB A safety mechanism that has been built into bitcoin is that freshly mined coins cannot be spent until they have 100 confirmations [81]. This prevents coins disappearing if a naturally resolved fork happens on a chain effectively disappears.

This is how Bitcoin Cash came into being, and why each holder of Bitcoin Core, up until the 1st August 2017 when the chains forked,

---

[81] Block maturation time, https://bitcoin.stackexchange.com/questions/1991/what-is-the-block-maturation-time, Accessed at Saturday, 25 January 2020

was a holder of equal count of Bitcoin Core and Bitcoin Cash when the chains forked.

But why did Bitcoin Cash fork away from Bitcoin Core? What made a certain percentage of the nodes within the network decide to run different versions of the bitcoin software implementing different consensus rules? The split was over scaling.

On-Chain Scaling

Early in bitcoin's history some people who ran bitcoin compliant software would do things like sending bitcoin from one wallet to another, back and forth, over and over, filling up the blocks in the block-chain. At one point it was free to send bitcoin, and so there was no loss to anyone doing so; they would do it just for fun or to maliciously mess with the network. In order to stop these types of things from happening, a fee structure was introduced to bitcoin, and where if anyone tried to send bitcoin back and forth repeatedly, they would only be able to send less and less until their bitcoin was consumed in fees.

To dissuade similar attacks on the network, Nakamoto also introduced a one megabyte (1 MB) cap on the size of each block of transactions. This limited the number of transactions in any one block and stopped any one malicious node from flooding the network with spurious transactions.

The problem with 1 MB blocks is that with a limited number of transactions in each block, naturally two things would happen. Firstly, in order for any one miner (or *full node*) in the network to earn any money the transaction fees gleaned from each block would need to in some way help match the electricity cost of mining each block to make any profit to incentivise the miner to bother processing the block. Of course miners made money by receiving new bitcoin with each new block they produced as well. But, with a limited number of transactions, and more and more computational power required to mine each block as more miners competed for rewards, the higher the transaction fees would need to be to compensate the miners. The second problem is that if bitcoin became very popular, then the number of transactions per second of the day would increase, but with a 1 MB limit on each block, the blocks would become full, and a backlog of transactions would ensue.

We have seen that the very first response that Nakamoto received on publishing her white-paper was a warning that scaling bitcoin would be a difficult proposition. So warnings of the issues of scaling were present from the very beginning of Bitcoin.

A simple solution to the problem of scaling, one would naturally think, would be to increase the size of each allowable block in the block-chain. But this met with resistance from the bitcoin community that grew to some size.

One of the primary reasons for the resistance was because 1 MB blocks allowed for nearly any computer with access to reasonable internet bandwidth to mine bitcoin as a *full node*. Every 10 minutes the mining computer would need to download a new block of transactions and at 1 MB every 10 minutes that did not seem too much burden on a mining node. This argument is largely ridiculous because running the bitcoin software as a full node on a computer that is not relatively powerful and not mining in association with many other computers as a combined pool (as one large full node), adds no value to the network as that computer would likely never win the Proof of Work competition.

The other cause for resistance was that of supposed purity of the vision of Bitcoin. The more mining nodes that supported the Bitcoin network the more decentralised the network would be and the harder for governments to shut down bitcoin. If block sizes increased beyond the capacity for small scale miners to manage, then the network would become more centralised and increase the risk that Bitcoin could be shut down. That is the theory at least.

Nakamoto, even within days of releasing the Bitcoin white paper, saw things differently. Nakamoto always saw a future where dedicating and professional mining farms of computers would run the network; where mining would be out of reach of home computers running in someone's garage, bedroom or office [82]. Nakamoto left scant clues as to his innermost thoughts, but the follow through of that proposition is that if mining farms established themselves widely enough across the globe and in different countries, it would be difficult for governments of the world to coordinate themselves to shut down bitcoin.

For the first few years of Bitcoin the scaling debate was rather hypothetical, because Bitcoin simply had not attracted enough business, and subsequent transactions, to warrant increasing the block size or worrying about scaling beyond planning for it in the future.

The debate literally went on for years. Those who saw Bitcoin as a truly disruptive technology to the incumbent banking institutions argued that not acting on scaling was tantamount to planning to fail. Those who were happy with eventual higher fees were happy to see things stay stagnant.

The option to simply increase block sizes within the blockchain came to be known as *on-chain scaling,* where one other proposal to scaling Bitcoin was to process the eventual high volume of transactions in another *side-chain* separate from Bitcoin and use the Bitcoin chain as some sort of settlement layer much the way that banks settle intra-bank payments within settlement systems separate from each banks transaction ledger software.

To satisfy the miners, transaction fee rules were introduced such that if ever a backlog of transactions occurred, the sender of Bitcoin could elect to increase the fee for their transaction to bump their transaction higher within the queue. The more you paid, the more likely you were to even to be able to use the network. It seems almost crazy that such things would happen,

---

[82] Nakamoto's notes on Bitcoin scaling, www.metzdowd.com, http://www.metzdowd.com/pipermail/cryptography/2008-November/014815.html, Accessed at Monday, 5 November 2018

given that high fees would scare off business, but you can see a long-winded explanation of transaction fee algorithm at the following address: https://en.bitcoin.it/wiki/Transaction_fees

As an idea of how ludicrous things became, a website was set up such that people could view how many transactions were *waiting* to be included in a block on the Bitcoin block-chain. You can view the website at https://www.blockchain.com/btc/unconfirmed-transactions

NB The site no longer shows how many transactions are waiting in the cue, just a list of transactions, presumably because sometimes it reaches into the tens, if not hundreds, of thousands of transactions; requiring correspondingly higher fees to be accepted into the ledger. Self updating, the website used to show new transactions as they arrived at a mining node, and how big the pool of transactions was in the queue, waiting to be processed.

This site shows where the number of transactions waiting in the queue rose to more than 250,000 https://jochen-hoenicke.de/queue/#0,all , where at that time it cost more than U.S. $50 to process a transaction even if that transaction was for a $2 cup of coffee.

To condense 9 years of debate into one sentence, the Bitcoin unconfirmed transaction queue grew in late 2017 to over 100,000 transactions, with little hope of some transactions making it into the blockchain without paying high fees for the transaction; this practically crippled the Bitcoin network from an economic point of view.

This was The Great Scaling Debate. The debate ended on 1st August 2017 with the advent of Bitcoin Cash, which was not enough to save Bitcoin Core, which then saw its exchange rate drop from US $20,000 per bitcoin down to around $3000 today. People just lost interest in Bitcoin Core. The transaction throughput of Bitcoin Core never recovered, as the following chart shows [83]:

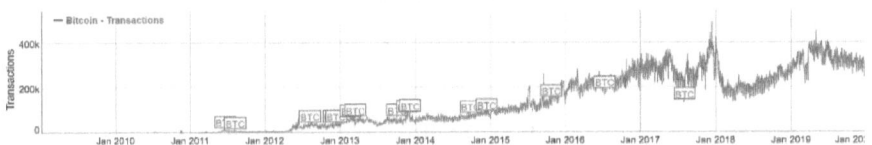

The peak is December 2017. The steady rise, reflecting steady rise in adoption of bitcoin, is more or less constant before that date. After December 2017, whenever the number of Bitcoin Core transactions gets high, the fee price increases and people balk away from using the Bitcoin Core network. To Bitcoin Cash advocates the evidence is clear; those running the Bitcoin Core network throttled the network and interest in Bitcoin Core.

The Bitcoin Trifecta

Any successful business knows that customers have to come first. Customers are the lifeblood of commerce and without them things come to an abrupt halt. But deciding *just who is your customer* seems to have been difficult for some within the bitcoin sphere.

With a currency, customers are obviously those who use the currency in their day-to-day lives, either for personal use or commercially. Commerce in some form will always exist regardless of which currency customers use, but for a currency to flourish it must have qualities that are attractive to customers. We dedicated a whole chapter to *"What is Money"* and what makes it useful, here we simply acknowledge that anyone wishing to fulfil the role of *currency creator* need put their customers first.

As with most dynamic systems an economy needs to find a healthy and symbiotic relationship between interacting parties in order to be stable, let alone flourish. Commerce, after all, is a process of give and take. Merchants provide goods and services,

---

[83] Source, Bitinfocharts, https://bitinfocharts.com/comparison/bitcoin-transactions.html, Accessed at Friday, 24 January 2020

and customers compensate merchants with currency when they purchase those goods and services. Currency, as a product, is an interesting beast though, for is not a merchant also a customer?

Bitcoin is even more interesting for as far as I can see there are three parties that need to be happy within the symbiosis for bitcoin to survive. There must be three winners in each transaction, and I call this the Bitcoin Trifecta.

Customers

Miners   Developers

The Bitcoin Trifecta

Customers are the most important and so are at the top of the trifecta, and must come first. This includes those using the currency as a merchant.

Miners and software developers must also win within the trifecta, but their places of second and third are interchangeable.

Together, customers, miners and developers form the Bitcoin Trifecta.

A *trifecta* in horse racing is a bet that can be placed on having selected the first, second and third place winners in a race. Picking all three as winners in any order is a *boxed trifecta*. The payout is usually high to the punter because of the unlikely odds of actually picking the winning combination.

If all other currencies of the world are in the same horse race as Bitcoin, then those who back a bitcoin currency not only have to urge bitcoin's customers, miners and developers to be winners, but also winners against all other currencies of the world!

Miners need to be rewarded for the cost of their computers and electricity they consume, developers need to be rewarded for the effort they put into software development and above all, customers must be rewarded with the most useful and cost effective currency available. Quite obviously if customers are not rewarded with benefits, they will flock to other currencies and the trifecta collapses.

Miners are rewarded with new bitcoin and transaction fees, but the question is, *"Do miners see developers as their customer?"* Bitcoin software developers rely on miners to use their code, so miners are definitely a customer of developers within the symbiosis, but what if any service does a miner feel they offer a developer? What loyalty does a miner owe a developer? It is obvious that they need each other for Bitcoin to survive, but what motivation does a miner have to reward a developer?

The answer has to be that rewarding the developer to make software that ultimately rewards users of Bitcoin has to be, in turn, rewarding back to the miner.

But what if the developers are incompetent and incapable of making suitable software that rewards users of Bitcoin? What if Bitcoin's developers do not have the prerequisite business and economic sense to make currency software that adequately fulfils the role of a successful currency?

These are all serious questions and ultimately lead to the question, *"Who is beholden to whom within the Bitcoin Trifecta?"* Is there a power imbalance within the trifecta and what can be done about it?

Never put quite within those words within the Bitcoin community the central gist of The Great Scaling Debate rotated around those issues.

Ultimately this debate was influenced by politics, economic view point and, like with any currency, came down to influences of power. Within Bitcoin Core this led to a distasteful coup, and we look at that now.

Open Debates, Closed Doors

Because software solutions like Bitcoin are 'open-source' and where anybody on Earth can view and take copies of the software such that the process of reviewing the stability, efficiency, security and validity of that code is public, you would think that the whole process of maintaining and modifying that code was democratised, but that, as we will investigate, turns out to be a pipe dream. Only certain people have access to modify the code and everyone is beholden to those people on many levels.

For example, the Bitcoin Core software is stored at www.github.com and freely available to the public. But only certain people have access to make modification to the code, and the circle of people allowed to modify that code is tight. While that may be reasonable from a security and quality standpoint, the undeniable affect is to introduce politics into the mix. It is not about software alone, it is about people, their personalities and ambitions.

The politics of those that maintain the software play a role in what they create and deliver. Beyond what ideological persuasions they have, financial incentive plays a role in what software they create and deliver when it comes to cryptocurrencies; after all the core business is *money*.

Beholden to the developers

Because Bitcoin is data and software rolled into one system amalgamating in currency, Bitcoin is 100% beholden to the developers of the software that manages the data. Questions should be asked of those developers.

Have they tested the code thoroughly? Are they aware of all the security implications of the changes that they make to the code? Do they actually know what they are doing? Or are they incompetent geeks who want to make a name for themselves? Are they professional in the way that they handle disputes as to the roadmap for the software? Do they have an ulterior motive for the changes they make to the code?

All of these questions are serious, and it is naive at best to not consider these things if you have money tied up in a cryptocurrency.

At least with a traditional bank you can be sure that errant players (whatever that means in context) will have their employment terminated, with the commercial imperative to have seamless and effortless payments driving that decision. Who terminates the employment of an errant Bitcoin developer?

Where developers in the Bitcoin arena are often and essentially their own boss, Bitcoin is beholden to developers.

Beholden To Miners

When the Bitcoin software is developed and tested by developers, someone has to run that software to make the whole system work. Bitcoin Miners fulfil this role. Miners are incentivised to run the software by receiving newly issued bitcoin and transaction fees, and so have a profit motive. Does that profit motive include doing what is right for Bitcoin even if it entails short-term losses and long-term gains such as increasing the block size?

While the Great Scaling Debate rates, even if developers unilaterally decided to increase the block-size of Bitcoin, there were literally thousands of miners whose buy-in must be gained in order for there to be any change to Bitcoin. Miners cannot be forced to run software that they do not want to run.

This is actually one of the biggest strengths, and biggest weaknesses of Bitcoin. A consensus model that is beholden to a disperse group of miners is on the one hand powerful, because it means that Bitcoin is adverse to manipulation be any one party. But the Nakamoto consensus model is also a weakness because it makes Bitcoin very brittle. Either all the miners move to a new version of the Bitcoin software incompatible with the previous version, or the blockchain splits and a new currency is created, devaluing the first.

No matter how it is looked at, Bitcoin is beholden to miners.

The Coup that should make people think

When Nakamoto left Gavin Andresen in charge of the bitcoin project he felt that he was leaving bitcoin in good hands. We know from history that Andresen cared passionately about bitcoin and went as far as co-founding The Bitcoin Foundation, a non-profit organisation dedicated to promoting bitcoin and furthering the technology of Bitcoin.

Andresen, whether he likes it or not, became quite a public figure and many videos of Andresen sharing the story of and generally discussing bitcoin are available on the internet. For all intents and purposes Andresen comes across as a quietly spoken gentleman. Obviously gifted with the intelligence that allowed him to win the merit of Nakamoto's favour, Andresen carried the Bitcoin software development effort for a number of years. Andresen headed up the open-source bitcoin project.

The political issue a running an open-source software project is the central thesis of this book, and is the issue that Andresen undoubtedly faced...*who do you trust with helping you with the software? Who do you trust with developing software for a global currency?*

You see, proponents of bitcoin will tell you that with bitcoin you do not trust in banks or governments but rather in mathematics and software that implements that mathematics. The rules of bitcoin, such as a 21 million bitcoin limit, are embedded in the software and are very hard to change. To change the mathematics of bitcoin, every bitcoin miner must agree on the software changes that implement the mathematical changes. If someone wanted to change core aspects of bitcoin, then all miners must agree on that change.

But the converse is actually the truth. The miners actually rely on the software programmers. Sure, they get the final say in what happens with what software they run, but they can only run the software that is provided to them.

It is not right to think of the relationship between bitcoin developers and miners as symbiotic. If programmers act in the best interest of miners, what incentive is there for miners to act in the best interest of programmers? Miners simply care that they are making money. Some, if not most miners would have little knowledge of the intricacies of the software they are running. Most would simply run the software they are provided. For those that take an interest in the overall economics of bitcoin, what real say do miners have in influencing developers?

Some attempts were made over the years to introduce voting rights of Bitcoin Core miners, such that miners could vote over what features went into new versions of the bitcoin software. But those efforts were either abandoned or the vote ignored by the developers. The developers held the true power and they knew it.

Contrast this to how normal projects are usually run within companies. Marketing types come up with the new ideas for products and they take their ideas to product developers who develop the product to their satisfaction. The successful of the marketing types are those that listen to their customers, and work with their developers to develop what the customers wants. Of course, if the developer does not live up to the company's expectations, the company will just find a new developer and get rid of the non-performing developer.

But what happens if there are no suitable marketing type persons in the mix? What happens if the developers effectively run the show? What happens if the developers think that miners are their customers rather than the people who use a currency? What if those in charge have no idea who their real customer is? What if the developers stage a coup and decide they know better than the marketing types?

Bitcoin is an interesting beast. Unlike most products were the cost of the product equates to money, money is the product when it comes to bitcoin. In that respect, those that control the currency need all the nous of the most sophisticated economist. They need to understand supply and demand of money. They need to know the lessons of those currencies that have failed in the past. They need to know what makes a currency successful.

Software developers, on the whole, are not renowned for being economists, and vice versa. It is a rare person who shares equal portions of both skills. It is even rarer to find a software developer who is both those and a manager of people. Add that to the rarity of the same person being a marketer.

But this is the position that Gavin Andresen found himself in when left with running the bitcoin software project. His job was to recruit people to help develop the bitcoin software, keep the economic vision of bitcoin alive, develop software and help with the marketing effort.

It was a big ask of anyone really, and it was not like Andresen applied for the position. Nakamoto dumped the position on Andresen when Nakamoto left the project.

We know from history that Andresen did his best. Andresen brought others in to assist with the software development effort. He started The Bitcoin Foundation, played the role of mentor and people manager, and in keeping Nakamoto's vision alive, did his best to maintain the economic philosophy behind bitcoin.

In bringing people on board to assist with the software effort, Andresen made some critical errors, errors in trust. Errors in trust are forgivable. Anyone can probably relate to having made an error in trust. But is a project personnel structure that is more or less guided by technology and developers forgiving? One has to feel sorry for Andresen, because the very confine of a software repository within an open-source project was to spell his demise within the Bitcoin Core sphere.

A crucial mistake

In order that if Andresen was ever hit by the proverbial bus, Andresen granted extra permissions to the bitcoin software repository to other developers. If anything happened to Andresen, others had access to the ability to change and manage the bitcoin software; and critically some had the ability to kick people off the repository if they wanted to, even Andresen.

And that is what happened. Andresen put his trust in people and his reward was to be booted off the Bitcoin Core project.

Let us look a little more closely at what happened, and examine the cautionary tale, which is twofold...be careful of who you trust, and, at the macro-scale, do not believe that bitcoin is a trustless system. Trust is built-in at every level of bitcoin, and you must trust in the developers of the software before trusting in anything else about the currency.

Mid way through 2011 Andresen invited Wladimir van der Laan to help out with writing code for the Bitcoin repository. How that invitation occurred is unclear, but it is safe to say that van der Laan somehow impressed Andresen enough such that he was trusted to modify the Bitcoin software. Such invitations are not uncommon in open-source projects, but rather par for the course. If you need backup and security in numbers, in case that proverbial bus hits, you need to trust someone. Andresen trusted van der Laan.

Other developers, such a Greg Maxwell were bought on board, and under Andresen's management things seemed to go well for Bitcoin. Over Andresen's tenure as the core maintainer of the Bitcoin software the price of Bitcoin grew from about U.S. $1 per bitcoin to over U.S. $400 per bitcoin, an astronomical increase by any standard. Whether the price of bitcoin would have increased without Andresen's stewardship is debatable, but Andresen's calm demure and inclusive nature most likely helped considerably.

Beyond managing a team of developers, Andresen had to deal with the regulatory issues of Bitcoin. Publicly Andresen supported regulation of Bitcoin, stating that regulation would be beneficial for the nascent technology [84].

All the while, Andresen grew the Bitcoin development team, and at some stage Andresen recruited the services of Wladimir van der Laan. It seems however that Andresen was a hands-off manager, and in 2014 Andresen stepped down as the lead developer of Bitcoin and actually handed over the reins to van der Laan [85] [86].

Both Andresen and van der Laan had become full time employees of The Bitcoin Foundation, with Andresen as the chief scientist. One imagines that Andresen was content playing a symbolic role of leader while concentrating on promoting Bitcoin and furthering

[84] Andresen speaks on Bitcoin regulation, (1/1/2014), "The Bitcoin Phenomenon", SQ1.tv, https://www.youtube.com/user/SQ1television, Accessed at Tuesday 6 November 2018

[85] Andresen hands over the reins to Wladimir van der Laan, https://en.bitcoinwiki.org/wiki/Wladimir_van_der_Laan, Accessed at Tuesday, 6 November 2018

[86] List of Bitcoin Core maintainers, www.bitcointalk.org, https://bitcointalk.org/index.php?topic=1774750.0, Accessed at Tuesday, 5 November 2018

the technology. A 'hands-off' manager, it seems that Andresen was happy delegating work to others, and trusting that his role within the Bitcoin team was respected.

Handing over the reins to van der Laan pretty much entailed handing over the keys to the Bitcoin repository on Github.com where the repository was now kept, and lifting van der Laan's privileges within the open-source project. Andresen kept his *maintainer* role within the repository, but van der Laan was also a maintainer, Andresen's peer.

In the background of Bitcoin becoming the phenomena that it became, there was always the scaling debate. Positions on each side of the debate grew entrenched over time, but it was clear from the statements made by Andresen that Andresen was in favour of simply increasing the block-size of Bitcoin so that the network could process more transactions [87]. Gregory Maxwell, whose profile within the Bitcoin community grew over his tenure, also supported a block-size increase [88].

By accepting employment with The Bitcoin Foundation part of the Bitcoin Trifecta had been solved, for Andresen and van der Laan at least. Their development work was being rewarded financially. Andresen also found himself advisory work to commercial operations making a dollar from Bitcoin [89]. Their time investment in Bitcoin was now being rewarded fiscally and they had money coming in. This must have relieved the inevitable pressure of computer programming without payment that Bitcoin developers

---

[87] Andresen supports increasing the Bitcoin block-size, "DevCore Boston 2015 | What Satoshi Didn't Know", Bitcoin Foundation, https://www.youtube.com/watch?v=rQ3e1Pzu7iI, Accessed at Tuesday 6 November 2018

[88] Greg Maxwell supports a Bitcoin block-size increase, https://lists.linuxfoundation.org/pipermail/bitcoin-dev/2015-December/011865.html, Accessed at Tuesday 6 November 2018

[89] Andresen becomes advisor to CoinBase (12/12/2013), Coinbase Raises $25 Million From Andreessen Horowitz, Coinbase, www.coinbase.com, https://blog.coinbase.com/coinbase-raises-25-million-from-andreessen-horowitz-3d25ab0f2d08, Accessed at Thursday, 8 November 2018

faced. But what about other developers such as Maxwell? How did they intend to be renumerated for their development effort?

In 2014, Greg Maxwell and another Bitcoin Core developer, Pieter Wuille, found a solution. Along with some others, related to Bitcoin one way or another, started their own company, Blockstream, and went to market to receive venture capital. Blockstream was successful in this endeavour and raised tens of millions of dollars in venture capital to fund their company [90]. But what product were venture capitalists investing in with Blockstream? Bitcoin is an open-source peer-to-peer system that rewards miners, not developers. What was Blockstream's pitch to investors?

It turns out that the pitch was to develop *side-chains* to the Bitcoin network/blockchain and where money could be made from these side projects. One such idea, the Lightning Network, was to develop a system of sending money over the internet completely separate from Bitcoin, and only use the Bitcoin network to settle accounts between nodes on this separate network. A future commercial product of Blockstream, Liquid, was sold to exchanges to settle bitcoin transactions quickly off the slow Bitcoin Core network.

Never having been realised, the Lightning Network is widely ridiculed as a failed project, but the die had been cast. Here were a group of Bitcoin Core developers actively developing technology to take business away from Bitcoin miners, and break the Bitcoin Trifecta. Side-chains that settle transactions off the bitcoin blockchain eat directly into mining fees and with bitcoin mining rewards halving every four years miners would rely more and more on fees. If miners of Bitcoin Core were ultimately greedy in supporting a network that compromised customers with high fees, developers starting their own company to rob miners of those fees was another story again. Bitcoin Core was in a world of trouble.

---

[90] Mosaic Ventures invests in Blockstream (22/02/2016), "Our Investment in Blockstream", https://www.mosaicventures.com/mosaicblog/2016/2/4/our-investment-in-blockstream, Accessed at Tuesday, 6 November 2018

What came next was to surprise everyone and forever taint the Bitcoin Core network.

Satoshi Nakamoto returns

In December 2015 the unexpected happened. Wired magazine broke a story based on supposedly leaked evidence that Satoshi Nakamoto was a computer scientist living in Australia named Craig Wright. The story was a bit of a bombshell with a collection of seemingly authentic documents and emails in support of the claim. The documents were also leaked to the Gizmodo magazine, which had no choice but to publish their story on the same day [91] [92].

It was not the first time reporters announced that they had found the person most likely to be Satoshi Nakamoto. More than a year earlier Newsweek reported having found a man actually called Satoshi Nakamoto and who, in their eyes, fit the description of the mythical Nakamoto of Bitcoin fame [93]. A story later lampooned as being a poor effort of investigative journalism, Nakamoto denied the story through his attorney. Newsweek had simply found a scientist and mathematician called Satoshi Nakamoto.

So what made the new stories any different?

The short answers is that the Wired and Gizmodo stories raised a lot of questions about the business dealings of Craig Wright, with

---

[91] Greenberg A., Branwen G. (08/12/2015), Bitcoin's Creator Satoshi Nakamoto Is Probably This Unknown Australian Genius, Wired, https://www.wired.com/2015/12/bitcoins-creator-satoshi-nakamoto-is-probably-this-unknown-australian-genius/, Accessed at Thursday, 8 November 2018

[92] Biddle S., Cush A. (09/12/2015), This Aussie Says He And His Friend Invented Bitcoin, Gizmodo, https://www.gizmodo.com.au/2015/12/this-australian-says-he-and-his-dead-friend-invented-bitcoin/, Accessed at Thursday, 8 November 2018

[93] Goodman L. (06/03/2014), The Face Behind Bitcoin, Newsweek, https://www.newsweek.com/2014/03/14/face-behind-bitcoin-247957.html, Accessed at Thursday, 8 November 2018

a seemingly large problem on his hands with the Australian Taxation Office and verifiable connections with Bitcoin related companies; but because many of the leaked documents were not verifiable the stories raised intrigue but not the verifiable proof that would convince the die-hard cypherpunks associated with Bitcoin.

Co-founder and then chairman of the Bitcoin Foundation, Peter Vessenes, said of Nakamoto in a Bitcoin documentary released by SQ1.tv in 20014 that, *"Satoshi exists…in the Bitcoin subconscious…things are named after him. It'll be like finding out who Santa Claus really is if Satoshi is ever revealed"* [94] and this mythical quality of Nakamoto seemed to serve Bitcoin with a creation myth that only helped the Bitcoin story. There was nobody to which to point a finger at, with all the faults of a human presence. Nakamoto held reverence for Bitcoin's invention and that reverence carried weight in the Bitcoin community.

It is hard to know Andresen's exact thoughts on hearing of the Wired and Gizmodo reports of having found Nakamoto, but we know from various sources that Andresen was keen to meet Nakamoto [93]. We also know that Andresen was reported to have said that *"Satoshi can have write access to the github repo[sitory] any time he asks."* [95] [96] That is, Andresen would be happy for Nakamoto to take control of the Bitcoin project should ever Nakamoto return.

---

[94] Peter Vessenes speaks about Satoshi Nakamoto, The Bitcoin Phenomenon,SQ1.tv, https://www.youtube.com/watch?v=6pWblf8COH4, Accessed at Thursday, 8 November 2018

[95] van der Laan's comments on Andresen, (08/11/2018), Bitcoin project blocks out Gavin Andresen over Satoshi Nakamoto claims, The Guardian, https://www.theguardian.com/technology/2016/may/06/bitcoin-project-blocks-out-gavin-andresen-over-satoshi-nakamoto-claims, Accessed at Thursday, 8 November 2018

[96] Reddit chatter about Andresen's views on Nakamoto, www.reddit.com, https://www.reddit.com/r/Bitcoin/comments/4hkvzz/gavin_andresen_satoshi_can_have_write_access_to/

The Guardian newspaper quoted van der Laan as complaining that Andresen would hand back control of bitcoin code to Nakamoto and it was van der Laan who in May 2016 staged a coup to take over Bitcoin development. It was a coup that shocked many, and arguably led to tens of billions of dollars being wiped from the value of Bitcoin. What happened?

Craig Wright reached out and contacted Gavin Andresen in early April 2016. It would appear that if Craig Wright was the real Satoshi Nakamoto and had been outed as such by the media, then Wright had very little to lose by reconnecting with the people who had shepherded Bitcoin in his absence. Why Wright would do that would later become apparent, but Wright was not denying the media stories, Wright was reaching out to Andresen as Satoshi Nakamoto.

The story of Andresen's eventual meeting with Wright in London is tabled in an article released by author Andrew O'Hagan in his 'The Satoshi Affair' and a reading of that article will prove more detailed than here [97]. For what has become common knowledge through the story telling of Gavin Andresen we share here.

That Andresen wanted to meet Wright is self-evident. Andresen accepted an invitation to fly to London for the meeting in early May 2016.

Meeting in a hotel, it had been arranged that Wright would provide cryptographic proof that he was Nakamoto, by digitally signing a message using the Bitcoin private-key for coins on the very first block of Bitcoin. This would show that Wright held those keys and must be Nakamoto.

Wright signed a message on a brand-new laptop computer, unboxed at the meeting, in order to prove that Wright was not in some way using tricks on a specially prepared computer. And with

---

[97] O'Hagan, A. (30/06/2016), The Satoshi Affair, London Review of Books, https://www.lrb.co.uk/v38/n13/andrew-ohagan/the-satoshi-affair, Accessed at Friday, 9 November 2018

that, to Andresen's mind, Satoshi had returned. Andresen had met the person who he admired and who had brought Bitcoin to the world.

On the 2nd of May 2016 Andresen wrote on his personal blog, *"I believe Craig Steven Wright is the person who invented Bitcoin."…"During our meeting, I saw the brilliant, opinionated, focused, generous – and privacy-seeking – person that matches the Satoshi I worked with six years ago"…"I am very happy to be able to say I shook his hand and thanked him for giving Bitcoin to the world."* [98]

Prophetically Andresen also wrote:

We love to create heroes – but also seem to love hating them if they don't live up to some unattainable ideal."…"I hope he manages to mostly ignore the storm that his announcement will create"

Andresen could not have been more right about a storm. Andresen's support for Wright immediately created a ripple throughout the world with the media and members of the Bitcoin community jumping on the story, and all too ready to attack Wright as a fraud.

The result?

Group dynamics is an interesting thing. How old is the story of the protégé usurping the master? Andresen had not counted on the politics of greed, paranoia and self preservation that was already incumbent within the Bitcoin Core development team. Andresen had allegedly said that Satoshi Nakamoto was welcome back to the Bitcoin team any time he wanted. Where did that leave Wladimir van der Lann now?

---

[98] Andresen lends support to Craig Wright being Satoshi Nakamoto, Andresen's personal blog, http://gavinandresen.ninja/satoshi, Accessed at Friday, 9 November 2018.

In a coup that was as swift as it was in its simplicity van der Laan revoked Andresen's maintainer privileges on the Bitcoin Github source code repository. In van der Laan's mind, van der Laan was the man in charge of Bitcoin development now, and no Satoshi Nakamoto was coming back to take his role. Andresen was not master of van der Laan any more.

We know that van der Laan knew the impact of his actions, as he brazenly broadcast his position on his own blog. In van der Laan's own words…

"When we saw the blog post convinced he found Satoshi, the prudent thing to do was to revoke his ownership of the 'bitcoin' organization on github, under which the Bitcoin Core repository currently lies, immediately.

In the past he has stated that "Satoshi can have write access to the github repo[sitory] any time he asks.", so if he is absolutely convinced that this is Satoshi, there is a risk that he'd give away the repository to a scammer….

Crossing the Rubicon

So when the question comes up whether we should make Gavin maintainer again, my answer, and that of many others is a resounding 'no'."[99]

The coup was complete. Bitcoin now had a suite of developers foreign to the seminal people who had steered Bitcoin through its first 8 years. Somehow, in denial, they aimed to preserve the creation myth of Bitcoin, but at the same time announce to the world that they were now in charge. Whether they aimed to form their own legendary status is not known, but we can be sure from their own words that power governed their actions.

---

[99] van der Laan justifies his coup, van der Laan's personal blog, https://laanwj.github.io/2016/05/06/hostility-scams-and-moving-forward.html, Accessed at Friday, 9 November 2018

That the coup was brewing for some time before May 2016 is evident in the things that were said after the event. Personal ambition of the usurpers aside, Andresen's support of Bitcoin being able to scale on-chain was quoted as one of the reasons Andresen was ousted. Andresen had been clear of his support for Bitcoin scaling to meet high demand, and that his efforts to achieve this was being subverted:

"[The Bitcoin block size may have to increase.] I may just have to throw my weight around and say, 'This is the way it's going to be. And if you don't like it, find another project.'", Andresen had said earlier, perhaps not realising the paranoia such statements would have on other Bitcoin developers [100].

"[Andresen] keeps repeating the 'block size must increase' line without being involved in any innovations that are happening," complained van der Laan." [99]

[Andresen says that] scaling [is] possible and easy, because why tell them it was going to take a long time and be complicated, right?" complained Bryan Bishop, another Bitcoin Core developer [99].

Power motive is one thing, profit motive is another. Debate rages to this day as to the profit motive of van der Laan, Bryan Bishop and other Bitcoin Core developers. Bitcoin was a maturing technology, Greg Maxwell and other Bitcoin Core developers had started their own company, Blockstream, to fund their development efforts and received millions of dollars in venture capital for the same. Blockstream's strategy was to develop *innovations* that would see Bitcoin Core's blockchain throttled at 1 MB blocks with side-chain technologies, such as the Lightning Network, processing most of the supposed Bitcoin Core transactions.

---

[100] Reutzel, B. (19/05/2017), Where is Gavin Andresen? The Quiet Exile of Bitcoin's Former Face, Coindesk, https://www.coindesk.com/where-is-gavin-andresen-the-quiet-exile-of-bitcoins-former-face/, Accessed at Friday, 9 November 2018

The central arguments of those pointing fingers at Blockstream surreptitiously taking over Bitcoin Core were, and still are:

1. Side-chain technologies will ultimately rob Bitcoin Core miners of transaction fees;

2. Blockstream controls van der Laan and is pushing for side-chain technologies [101]; and

3. Blockstream has investors that are either bankers or financially affiliated with bankers [102];

A whole book could be written about the connection of Blockstream to bankers, and how banking interests are the antithesis of Bitcoin, but we are interested here in Bitcoin Cash, not Bitcoin Core. Whatever the influence of bankers on throttling the Bitcoin Core network, and the control they have one way or another over Bitcoin Core developers, the economics of the decisions made by van der Laan and other Bitcoin Core developers ultimately led to Bitcoin Cash! Why?

It comes down to competency.

As early as 2015 Gavin Andresen spoke clearly on his thoughts that Bitcoin Core lacked suitable leadership [103] in respect development guidance. Ironically when he spoke of such things Andresen was speaking about his own failings as leader of Bitcoin Core. Widely regarded as a gentleman and of suitable intelligence to grapple with the technical problems of Bitcoin, Andresen

---

[101] Reddit chatter pointing to Blockstream controlling van der Laan, https://www.reddit.com/r/btc/comments/68wfx9/no_one_knows_who_is_payin g_wladimirs_salary_no_it/, Accessed at Saturday, 10 November 2018

[102] Reddit chatter on Bitcoin Core being co-opted by bankers, https://www.reddit.com/r/btc/comments/7d8pjq/blockstream_is_funded_by_the _bankers_that_bitcoin/, Accessed at Saturday, 10 November 2018

[103] Gavin Andresen admits to the leadership failings over Bitcoin Core, The Bitcoin Foundation, https://www.youtube.com/watch?v=0iQSRGT3nfE, Accessed at Saturday, 10 November 2018

lacked the capacity to rally the troops to his cause, especially when it came to scaling bitcoin.

After the 2016 coup that effectively silenced Andresen among the Bitcoin Core development elite who managed the software, things did not improve for bitcoin or its management, they began to fail. On the surface, it may have seemed that things were humming along just fine. The price of Bitcoin to the US Dollar rose from U.S. $450 in 2016 to U.S. $20,000 in 2017, in an exponential curve as more and more people around the world came to be aware of Bitcoin. This was the exact scaling of the network effect that people had warned of for years.

2017 proved to be a pivotal year for Bitcoin. The scaling debate raged on and nothing was done to increase the block size, allowing more transactions in each block. The online Bitcoin forums became forums for heated and toxic arguments over Bitcoin scaling. Blockstream focused their development efforts on the Lightning Network, which ultimately came to be referred to by one commentator as the Lightning *Not*work, because it never seemed to be finished, it never seemed to realise its dream of providing a scaling solution for Bitcoin [104].

Because of the transaction fee regime that developers had put in place to entrench a fixed 1 MB block size, by the end of 2017 Bitcoin Core fees skyrocketed to U.S. $50 per transaction, effectively crippling the network. The market collapsed and Bitcoin Core's dominance fell to 38% from over 80% on Andresen's 2016 outing.

If based on those metrics alone, the competency of the Bitcoin Core developers and those in charge of the Bitcoin network can rightly be called into question. With 100% starting dominance of Bitcoin Core, Bitcoin's reputation and capacity to maintain

---

[104] See Rick Falkvinge's range of videos on YouTube about the Bitcoin Scaling Debate and the Lightning Network, https://www.youtube.com/channel/UC8aCt-P8D9mU3CMjeKUWQwg/videos, Accessed at Saturday, 10 November 2018.

dominance by keeping relevant people, i.e. customers, happy was destroyed. It could be argued that Bitcoin Core developers were basically incompetent. It could be argued they were incompetent as developers and as economists.

In retrospect it is simple to understand why Bitcoin Core's market dominance fell to 38%. Other cryptocurrencies took the remaining share. None least of which is Bitcoin Cash. Bitcoin Core could have had it all, if its management had kept relevant people within the Bitcoin Trifecta happy. But they had failed [105].

In August 2017, fed up with Bitcoin Core's failure to address the scaling issues of Bitcoin, a percentage of the Bitcoin miners began running different Bitcoin software, Bitcoin Cash. And that is all it took, Bitcoin had forked into Bitcoin Core and Bitcoin Cash.

Bitcoin Cash software supported bigger block sizes. Without trivialising the effort required to write software, the scaling fix for Bitcoin thus far seems to have been as easy as that. Bitcoin Cash software supports up to 32 megabytes worth of transactions per block. In September 2018 as *Stress Test* was performed on the Bitcoin Cash network and over 2 million transactions were processed in one day, with one block processing over 25,000 transactions [106]. In November 2018, the Bitcoin Cash network processed multiple 32MB blocks from everyday transaction traffic [107], indicating that scaling of Bitcoin is not only necessary but that

---

[105] The Reddit forum community reacts to van der Laan's failed leadership, www.reddit.com, https://np.reddit.com/r/btc/comments/497ug6/the_official_maintainer_of_bitcoin_core_wladimir/, https://www.reddit.com/r/btc/comments/688b6s/who_is_wladimir_j_van_der_laan/, Accessed at Saturday, 10 November 2018.

[106] Partz, H. (02/09/2018), Bitcoin Cash Stress Test Results: 2.1 Million Transactions Cause No Surge in Fees, Coin Telegraph, https://cointelegraph.com/news/bitcoin-cash-stress-test-results-21-million-transactions-cause-no-surge-in-fees, Accessed at Sunday, 11 November 2018

[107] Redman, J. (11/11/2018), Bitcoin Cash Miners Break Records Processing Multiple 32 MB Blocks, news.bitcoin.com, https://news.bitcoin.com/bitcoin-cash-miners-break-records-processing-multiple-32-mb-blocks/, Accessed at Sunday, 11 November 2018

Bitcoin Cash proponents had made the right decision to scale bitcoin *on-chain*.

Contrast this with the Bitcoin Core network, which can process only a few thousand transactions in each block and which still has problems with transactions waiting around to be included in some block.

The Great Scaling Debate was settled with the creation of Bitcoin Cash. Arguably the lion's share of marketing power, computer science know-how and capacity to attract customers and merchants (still customers when it comes to currency) alike has moved to the Bitcoin Cash network, but Bitcoin Cash still has its problems. None least of which is that in early 2020 it is now the Bitcoin Cash developers who wish to be financially compensated for their work.

At the time of writing this paragraph, it is currently 132 times more expensive to process transactions on the Bitcoin Core network than it is the Bitcoin Cash network [108]. It is often around 16 times more costly to transact on Bitcoin Core than Bitcoin Cash, but as more people use Bitcoin Core the more expensive it is for customers to use the network.

With the Great Scaling Debate over, Bitcoin Cash had arrived and proponents believe with capacity to please customers. The rest, as they say, is history and which is still in the making.

Democratisation of Banking?

There seemed to be an undercurrent within the Bitcoin Core community which got upset by a notion that the average person cannot run a full mining node on their home-based personal computer, with the notion that without such home-based miners the Bitcoin Core network will become 'centralised'. What they

---

[108] Bitcoin Cash vs. Bitcoin Core statistics, https://cash.coin.dance/stats

mean by this is that they feared that Nakamoto Consensus will no longer work on the network because honest nodes may not control the majority of the mining function where fewer and fewer mining outfits have enough computing power to mine bitcoin.

There ultimately has to be a sad realisation to those that held this view, which is that at some point the Bitcoin Core database, the open ledger, would become so big, and the number of new transactions arriving at each full node that many, that personal home-based computers would simply be too inefficient to cope with the storage and internet bandwidth capacity required to maintain such a node, unless the network was throttled.

I can empathise with those people. Their underlying emotion is one of feeling left out and unimportant in the scheme of things.

Bitcoin probably felt democratic when the network first started, but those days have fallen well behind us. There is the obvious question, though, as to whether or not Bitcoin was ever democratic? Since when did the average person have any real say over the future direction of the network? Their efforts in securing the network were surely appreciated by all others, but their opinion probably did not really count.

Even now that Bitcoin Cash has separated from Bitcoin Core, there is no real notion of a democratic process going on in the decision making as to how the network is developed.

Some inroads have been made with the proposal of a Bitcoin Cash Standard Organisation [109], but this is only a proposal at this stage. Let us face it, even where organisations do have voting mechanisms, such as within The United Nations, the level of

---

[109] Yang, H. (31/08/2018), The Proposal of Establishing the Bitcoin Cash Standard Organisation, www.medium.com, https://medium.com/@yhaiyang/the-proposal-of-establishing-the-bitcoin-cash-standard-organization-bcso-157bb499d357, Accessed at Saturday, 10 November 2018

politicking in such organisations is only increased to a more centralised voting arena.

The Great Scaling Debate was over but the politics of winning the heart of customers was just starting.

The Killer Application for Bitcoin Cash - Money

A simple internet search shows people periodically ask *"what is the killer application for Bitcoin?"* What people mean by that question is *"What use of Bitcoin is going to make Bitcoin widely used throughout society?"*

It is an unusual question to ask, because obviously bitcoin's use as *money* is what bitcoin was designed to do. Surely that is the killer application. So why ask what bitcoin is going to be good for?

The answer is that bitcoin has not taken off as a mainstream currency across the globe. While there are pockets of aggregated and increasing usage, bitcoin has no mainstream recognition and widespread use right across the globe. There may be millions of people using bitcoin in the year 2020, but there are billions of people in the world and bitcoin is still a relatively unused currency.

Bitcoin Cash has significant advantages over Bitcoin Core which are arguably allowing it to win the war of the hearts and minds of a general populous, but in early 2020 the usage statistics of Bitcoin Cash has been flat for over a year and not growing at all; a year and a half after its separation from Bitcoin Core. Bitcoin Cash either needs to find common usage as an everyday currency or find its killer app.

The term *killer application* or *killer app* stems from the early days of the computer software industry, where successful and widely used applications could make the software's author a lot of money, *a killing* if you will. VisiCalc, the first spreadsheet software for personal computers, is an example of a killer app. Initially released in 1979, and with hundreds of thousands of copies sold, VisiCalc made a fortune for its creator, Software Arts.

Software such as Microsoft's Basic is another such example, with the widespread use of the software effectively launching Microsoft as one of the most successful companies of all time. It was, however, Microsoft's MS DOS software which became this most successful killer app of all time, being the basis operating system for personal computers over decades with sales in the hundreds of millions of copies.

Bitcoin Cash as Money

It sounds almost ludicrous to perceive of other uses for something called Bitcoin Cash than its use as money, but many other applications of the database behind the network have been thought of and are currently being trialled.

The Bitcoin Cash ledger is a database of financial transactions; each transaction storing information about how much bitcoin was spent, from whom and to whom. But extra information can be stored in the transaction data, such as messages, and that facility is being taken advantage of to provide novel services.

Before we look at other uses for Bitcoin Cash, let us look at where Bitcoin Cash is being successfully used as a currency.

Bitcoin and Travel

It seems that Bitcoin Cash may have a very useful function as money when it comes to travelling. How many times have you travelled to another country only to have to exchange your money from one currency to another? This, with exorbitant exchange fees charged each time you change your money from one currency to another.

Bitcoin Cash offers an alternative to this conundrum if and where you can spend Bitcoin Cash internationally, and stay within one currency.

In Australia a group of tourist operators and merchants have adopted Bitcoin Cash as not only a currency they accept but a hopeful drawcard for international tourists who are also cryptocurrency fans. Forming an ecosystem of sorts over there are now over 150 merchants of various descriptions accepting Bitcoin Cash in the North Queensland region of Australia. This may be extraordinary but is nothing compared with the congregation of merchants accepting Bitcoin Cash in Slovenia. Over 600 merchants now accept Bitcoin Cash in Slovenia, with the central idea of attracting people to the region and the ecosystem.

When viewed as just another currency, Bitcoin ATMs are now available in some airports, where you can exchange fiat currency for Bitcoin. Having bitcoin ATMs in airports not only supports those requiring the currency but is great marketing. Thousands to millions of people pass through busy airports and strategically placed bitcoin ATM machines is free advertising for bitcoin. In this respect the notion of bitcoin becoming an internationally recognised currency is making some impact.

The tipping point – Staying in the currency

If you travel internationally, then you will understand intuitively what I am about to say. If I travel to the United Kingdom from Australia, and need cash to spend in the UK, then I can exchange Australian dollars to British pounds (pound sterling) at the airport on arrival at the UK and do that for a cost of around 5% (exorbitant!). And then, of course, when I leave the UK, the British pound that I have in my wallet is next to useless when I return to Australia, so again at the airport I exchange the pound back to Australian dollars (at a cost of 5%. Exorbitant!). The foreign exchanges make a healthy living, while I lose out each time I exchange one currency for another.

But what happens if cryptocurrencies become so prevalent that rather than exchanging from a fiat currency to a cryptocurrency in order to perform some sort of transaction, I do (or can do) sufficient commerce in a cryptocurrency that it pays my way to always keep my stored value in that cryptocurrency? That cryptocurrency can then be seen to have come sufficiently of age that it has reached a tipping point of adoption that it effectively becomes a currency in its own right, despite protests from one or other government that it is 'not a currency'. The *travel* use case of bitcoin then becomes a stepping stone for those hoping to find the killer app for bitcoin.

That would be a tipping point, and it has been suggested that Bitcoin, in one of its forms, will one day become the new World Reserve Currency, usurping the U.S. dollar. It is a remarkable concept to think about, and a *bitcoin for travel* use case may promote this; but this author feels a concept that is farfetched at this stage. There are many problems with bitcoin that need overcoming before it would become anywhere near an international reserve currency. The chapter, Problems with Bitcoin Cash, addresses those problems. Let us look closer at using bitcoin for everyday use.

Bitcoin Debit Cards

Most of the world has already moved to electronic money. The Visa and MasterCard service providers maintain a massive electronic currency network that spans the globe. Nearly everyone in a modern progressive country that has a stable electricity and telecommunications network is familiar with using a credit or debit card to pay for goods and services electronically.

Those who aim to make an industry out of cryptocurrencies are well aware of the power the existing electronic currency networks exert by their very presence and as barriers to entry.

With the advent of a cryptocurrency such as Bitcoin Cash, capable of processing millions of transactions per day, there would be no impediment to taking on the business of all the merchants in the world who now accept the likes of cards provided by Visa and MasterCard. The central problem is that

Visa and MasterCard, and their elk, are not going to succeed their businesses easily and it is easier for merchants to work with the incumbents then to take a risk on working with a new and unproven technology such as Bitcoin Cash. The basic problem is that although dealing with electronic currency, the cards that Visa and MasterCard provide customers to prove that they have ownership of the currency are physical. The machines that merchants use to identify people and their money by use of cards are physical. And the physical infrastructure is simply too hard for merchants to change unless there is considerable economic benefit to do so.

So various cryptocurrency service providers have sought to partner with the likes of Visa to provide debit cards that are accepted by the current physical infrastructure, but which process the transaction behind the scenes as a cryptocurrency transaction.

One such company is FuzeX and the electronic debit card that they are producing will allow people to use the FuzeX debit card at existing EFTPOS (electronic funds transfer point of sale) machines across the world.

With these types of services there is certainly no impediment to the ready use of Bitcoin Cash as cash across the world, but for a basic problem. Solutions like the FuzeX card effectively exchange Bitcoin Cash for fiat currency at the point of sale, tapping into the existing finance infrastructure serviced by EFTPOS machines, but charge the consumer for the currency exchange. This puts a premium on using the card and the cryptocurrency. It effectively negates some of the ideological invention of bitcoin in the first place; especially when it comes to Bitcoin Cash which network prides itself on low fees. It is hard for this author to see how this use case would ever be a kipper app for Bitcoin Cash leading to mainstream adoption, but it is a stepping stone.

Other Uses of Bitcoin Cash

Other uses for the Bitcoin Cash network and underlying database have been found and are being explored, such as storing messages in the transaction records in the distributed ledger database such that those messages will be available for as long as the Bitcoin Cash network survives. www.memo.cash is one such initiative. The website for memo.cash is not very informative about how the system works. Presumably one creates a Bitcoin Cash wallet with memo.cash and pays a small fee per message that is posted to the blockchain. Looking at some of the newest posts on the site indicates to this author that the service is little used and is used predominantly for fun. The notion that the memos are *uncensorable* because the memos are distributed across the globe at Bitcoin Cash mining sites is novel and may have benefit for news prosperity.

A site, www.read.cash, allows users to submit articles that people can tip the author of the article with Bitcoin Cash. Still using Bitcoin Cash as money, the site allows for something unachievable with many other electronic money networks…the ability to send very small amounts of money. For instance, you can tip U.S. 20 cents and probably less. Achieving such small transactions with the Visa or MasterCard network would be impossible, and is made possible using Bitcoin Cash because of the very low fees for Bitcoin Cash payments.

To date, none of these applications would classify as a killer app, but if any one of the applications, or all combined, are successful, then Bitcoin Cash as an ecosystem would become a killer app in its own right.

More on Bitcoin Cash Wallets

Because the value of your Bitcoin Cash is stored on the network rather than actually in your electronic wallet, and because your electronic wallet may be vulnerable to theft or loss, there are ways of to effectively store your bitcoin away from your electronic wallet that reduces the potential for loss. There are also safeguards you can take to reclaim your wallet under most circumstances if you lose the device your electronic wallet is on.

A typical Bitcoin Cash wallet is simply an application on your smartphone or personal computer. What happens, for instance, if you lose your smartphone with your bitcoin wallet on it?

Mnemonic - 12 Word Backup of Your Private Key

You may see on your electronic wallet a button to press to *backup* your wallet. This is a misnomer; you do not back up any data of your wallet. All that that button does is take you through a simple process that generates a mnemonic, which is a set of words for you to write down and store safely somewhere. The mnemonic is commensurate with the private key of your wallet and subsequent funds held on the Bitcoin Cash network. With it you can reclaim your wallet and access to your bitcoin, on another device.

The following is a sample mnemonic:

```
body decision painful space bloom sunlight grown vein son
third mirror dance
```

If you lose the device with your electronic bitcoin on it, but have your mnemonic saved safely somewhere, you can use that mnemonic in another electronic bitcoin wallet to reclaim the bitcoin that was associated with the lost wallet.

Of course, if your device with an electronic bitcoin wallet is stolen and the thief gains access to the wallet, the thief may be able to transfer the bitcoin to a bitcoin address of their own, and you will not be able to reclaim the bitcoin with a mnemonic. The same is true if your electronic device is somehow hacked and the bitcoin stolen.

Paper and Hardware Wallets

If you had a bitcoin wallet on your mobile phone and you lost your phone or it was stolen, you may well have lost the bitcoin associated with that wallet. This might not be a big deal if you only had U.S. $50 associated with the wallet, but if you had a wallet with U.S. $10,000 of associated bitcoin, then that may well be a catastrophe to you.

For this reason, or where you may want to have multiple bitcoin wallets, you can print out a *paper wallet* on a piece of paper, or purchase what is known as a *hardware wallet*.

Paper Wallets

A paper wallet is quite literally a piece of paper with bitcoin keys printed on it; usually printed from a personal computer. Bitcoin requires what is known as a *public key* (a set of letters and numbers) that people can send bitcoin to, and a *private key* which allows you to set up an electronic bitcoin wallet from which to send and receive bitcoin.

It might sound funny that you can send money to a piece of paper, but when you send bitcoin to a paper wallet you actually send bitcoin to the public key address of the wallet on the public and distributed bitcoin ledger. If you keep the private key printed on the paper wallet a secret then only you can retrieve the bitcoin stored, effectively, *on* the paper wallet. Effectively, however, the bitcoin is stored on the network as if the bitcoin network were an electronic bank.

You can find web pages that generate Bitcoin Cash paper wallets at the following web addresses:

https://www.bitcoincash.org/wallets.html

https://paperwallet.bitcoin.com/

NB WARNING – Even though some web sites allow you to generate a paper wallet while still online, the safest way to generate a wallet is to download the html page and run the code on the html page that generates the wallet on a personal computer that is not connected to the internet and print to wallet on a printer that is not connected to the internet. This is the least of your precautions. You should only generate a wallet using html code from a source that you trust. The risk that you run is that the html page, your computer or printer are compromised in some way that the private key generated is sent (over the internet) to a malicious actor such that if you deposit funds to the public key of the wallet, the malicious actor has the private key and can steal those funds. So take the warnings seriously and take precautions commensurate with the amount of money you want to deposit onto the paper wallet and the level of risk that you are comfortable with, with your bitcoin.

Paper wallets can be stored in a safe place and used as your own private bank account, as much as bitcoin is private. Or you can send bitcoin to the public key address on a paper wallet and give the paper wallet to someone as a gift. They can redeem the bitcoin associated with the paper wallet using the private key, onto their own electronic wallet.

The obvious drawback with paper wallets is that they can also be lost, or even accidentally burned in a fire. The private key in the wallet can be written down somewhere else and kept safely away from the paper wallet, of course. But then, of course, you must keep that copy of the private key safe and secure also.

Hardware Wallets

Hardware wallets are electronic devices with a software bitcoin wallet running on them. So why isn't your smartphone a hardware wallet if it runs a bitcoin wallet software? The answer is that hardware wallets are specifically built to run cryptocurrency wallets and usually run no other software than the wallet. In this way the hardware wallet aims to minimise the chance of the electronic device being hacked.

While the best endeavours of smartphone manufacturers and smartphone operating system providers, such as Apple Computer, to prevent malicious software being downloaded to the smartphone, the internet is full of stories of rogue or Trojan software accidentally being downloaded to a smartphone, compromising the security of the smartphone itself. Some smartphones are safer than others, but if you run a bitcoin wallet software on your smartphone there may be a chance that the wallet may be compromised and your bitcoin stolen. It depends entirely on the quality of the bitcoin wallet software, security wise, and the means by which your smartphone is secured against malicious attack.

Bitcoin relies 100% on the owner of the bitcoin being able to secure the private key to their bitcoin wallet. If the private key is lost or stolen, so too is access to the bitcoin stored against that key on the network. We cover the problems of bitcoin in the similarly named chapter, but here we ask the question, *Would you store U.S. $100,000 on your bitcoin wallet on your mobile phone?*

If you wouldn't risk that much money to your mobile phone, then that is the market that manufacturers of hardware wallets are targeting. The idea is that you effectively store your bitcoin on a device separate from your smartphone or personal computer, and you keep the hardware wallet safe somewhere. You can have a small amount of bitcoin on your smartphone wallet, and larger amounts on the hardware wallet, for example.

In like manner to a wallet for your smartphone, most hardware wallets allow you to write down a mnemonic for the hardware wallet, such that if the hardware device is lost, stolen or becomes unusable then there is a way to retrieve the bitcoin stored against that wallet, unless a thief moves the bitcoin to their own wallet etc.

Security is Paramount

Whether you have a bitcoin wallet on your smartphone or personal computer, or if you have a paper wallet or hardware wallet, it should be obvious by this stage of the book that the responsibility of keeping the private key to that wallet safe and secure rests squarely with you, the owner of the wallet.

Bitcoin wallets are not like traditional bank accounts. If you forget your password to your bank account, you may simply be able to ring up your bank and ask them to help you out by resetting the password. You might be able to achieve the same by walking into the nearest branch of your bank for assistance. The same is not true for bitcoin. If you lose access to your wallet key, or if the information is stolen, then there is nobody to go to for assistance. It is your responsibility 100% to maintain security over your bitcoin wallet.

This may be something that you would prefer. In some countries banks have collapsed and all of their customer's money has disappeared along with the bank. In some countries governments have seized money from citizens' bank accounts to help pay for government debt. Perhaps you simply do not want anyone to know the size of the assets you hold. For whatever reason you chose to hold bitcoin, however, security over the keys to the wallets you own is paramount.

Sending and Receiving Bitcoin Cash

It is extremely easy to send and receive Bitcoin Cash using a wallet application. I hesitate to say that it is easy to send and receive *money* using Bitcoin Cash because in some countries Bitcoin Cash is not recognised as legal tender. If you consider money to be whatever people consider money to be, then it is very easy to send and receive money using Bitcoin Cash.

The distributed and public ledger of the Bitcoin Cash network tracks how much BCH is available to a Bitcoin Cash wallet, and each wallet effectively shows you the balance available to send to another Bitcoin Cash wallet.

In this chapter we cover how to send and receive Bitcoin Cash.

Bitcoin Cash Addresses

A Bitcoin Cash wallet acts like a personal bank account in many respects, and has what is known as a Bitcoin Cash *receiving address* instead of having a bank account number to send funds to.

A Bitcoin Cash receiving address looks much like the below:

qqzt2v3nqvshrazf4lhfpsq2azjt7pczwyan43t4y3

If you have a Bitcoin Cash wallet, you can send BCH to that address.

The thing to note and remember about Bitcoin Cash receiving addresses is that they change each time you click on the [Receive] button on your wallet. The address changes each time you receive BCH so that the pseudo-anonymity of your wallet is preserved. Mathematically all of the different receiving addresses for a wallet are tied together and sending bitcoin to any one of the receiving addresses for a wallet effectively increments the balance of the wallet; even if the receiving address has been used before.

Anyone who has the inclination and the technical know-how to view data within the pubic BCH ledger can ultimately find out how much BCH you have in your wallet given the BCH address used to receive BCH, but the average person will not know how much BCH you have in your wallet, or even care. By changing the receiving address each time a wallet receives bitcoin, this makes it harder for someone to analysing the ledger to get an overall picture of transactions for that wallet. You can reuse previously displayed receipt addresses as they do not expire, but it is recommended to always use a newly presented receipt address as this will lessen the extent to which other people can see how much Bitcoin Cash you have in your wallet.

Sending Bitcoin Cash

From within the wallet software you can paste or type in a bitcoin cash receiving address of the wallet you would like to send bitcoin cash to, or most smartphone wallets support the scanning of what is called a QR Code, which looks like this:

You scan the QR code, which is a pictorial representation of a Bitcoin Cash address, and then proceed with sending the bitcoin.

Most wallets allow you to enter the amount of bitcoin cash you would like to send, or to enter the amount in a fiat currency such as Australian Dollars. The exchange rate is referenced from a server on the internet.

And that is all that is required. The fee for sending the bitcoin is largely automatically set by the wallet software itself, and is generally a very generous fee on the Bitcoin Cash network. Some wallets allow you to manually enter the fee you would like to pay to send the bitcoin.

Receiving Bitcoin Cash

Receiving bitcoin cash is as easy as sending bitcoin cash. All you need do is provide the sender your receiving address, or its equivalent QR Code, and the sender uses their bitcoin cash wallet to send the funds to the receiving address. There are no fees for receiving bitcoin cash.

Merchant Services

It is hard to imagine that Bitcoin Cash will make any inroads into becoming a useful economic tool without first having tailored solutions for merchants such that they can readily accept bitcoin cash as a method of payment.

There are many companies on the case, offering a variety of tools catering to the needs of merchants. A curated list of merchant applications for Bitcoin Cash and Bitcoin Core can be found at:

https://www.bitcoincash.org/accept-bitcoin-cash.html
or
https://www.bitcoin.com/merchant-solutions/

Two Primary Types of Bitcoin Merchant Applications

There are two primary types of bitcoin merchant applications; those which allow receipt of bitcoin at the point of sale, and which effect the transfer of bitcoin to the merchant's wallet, and those which allow a customer to pay in bitcoin, but which effect payment to the merchant in a fiat currency.

Bitcoin merchant applications (such as Bitpay) which effect payment to the merchant in fiat currency effectively act as an intermediary exchange and where the customer transfers bitcoin to the provider of the merchant application, and where the merchant application provider exchanges the bitcoin for fiat currency for a percentage fee (e.g. 1%), and transfers that fiat currency to the merchant's bank account. This requires establishing a relationship with the provider of the merchant application and providing the merchant's bank account details to the merchant application provider.

The second primary type of bitcoin merchant application effectively provides the merchant with half of a bitcoin wallet; one that allows bitcoin receipt, but no ability to send bitcoin. This is to overcome the bitcoin merchant conundrum. The *Bitcoin Cash Register* app for android or iOS smartphones is one such application.

The Merchant Conundrum

Setting up a Bitcoin Cash wallet on a PC, smartphone or tablet is easy, but a merchant must be aware that whoever has access to the private keys of that wallet also has direct access to the Bitcoin Cash on that wallet. The conundrum for merchants is that they need to have a tool that easily allows customers to make payment to a wallet, without giving private key access to the merchant's employees.

The easiest way to accept payment to a Bitcoin Cash wallet is just to have a picture of a QR Code pasted up at the point of sale at the merchant address. Customers can scan the QR Code with their Bitcoin Cash wallet and make payment to that address. The problem with this method is that it is not easy to determine if a particular payment has been made and which customer made which payment. For this reason, a dedicated merchant application is necessary and where the application tracks the transaction as it is made and lets the merchant know when any one particular transaction has made its way to the Bitcoin Cash network.

Many free bitcoin merchant applications exist and which effect this type of bitcoin merchant application. The advantage of this type of application for the Bitcoin Cash network, is that the only fee applicable to transactions is the Bitcoin Cash network fee (generally less than U.S. 1 cent) and where the customer pays that fee. That is, the cost to the merchant is nothing.

Zero Confirmation – The second conundrum

The second conundrum for merchants who wish to receive payment via Bitcoin Cash is a decision over at which point in time to accept that a transaction is locked down within the Bitcoin Cash blockchain.

When a transaction is made on the Bitcoin Cash network it is considered *confirmed* when the transaction has made its way into a mined block of transactions that has made its way onto the Bitcoin Cash blockchain, a linked chain of such blocks of transactions. Each time a new block of transactions is added to the blockchain, the number of confirmations that a transaction has increases by 1, and where that transaction is within an earlier block within the chain. Until the transaction makes its way to a block within the blockchain, the transaction has a confirmation number of 0 (zero), and is said to have Zero Confirmation.

For low cost transactions, such as payment for a cup of coffee, a merchant may decide to accept the payment as having been cleared with zero confirmation. For higher value transactions the merchant may wish to wait for the transaction to be embedded deeper within the blockchain and to have a higher confirmation number. The conundrum is that each block takes 10 minutes, on average, to be formed by the network and it is generally considered safe to feel that a transaction is locked into the blockchain after six confirmations…i.e. after one hour. How many customers are going to wait one hour for a merchant to feel safe that they have paid for a cup of coffee?

Take away – Zero Confirmation may be acceptable to some merchants and for the majority of their payment receipts. The higher the confirmation number the more confident the merchant should feel that the transaction is secured to the blockchain.

Because of the chance that a block of transactions may ultimately be rejected by the network a merchant should feel more confident of the validity of a transaction the more confirmations that a transaction has. A network that is widely mined and considered relatively secure, such as the Bitcoin Cash network, has little trouble getting each valid transaction on a block and the blockchain, but the level of risk taken be the merchant, as to the number of confirmations required before accepting payment, is up to the merchant.

An accepted number of confirmations before it is considered unlikely for a transaction to be rejected by the network is 6 confirmations (https://en.bitcoin.it/wiki/Confirmation), but the general rule of thumb to follow is that the deeper a transaction is within the blockchain, the more that transaction is tied to that blockchain, increasing the confidence held by the network that the transaction is valid.

Mining Bitcoin Cash

Bitcoin Cash transactions make their way into the Bitcoin Cash distributed, open ledger, and new Bitcoin Cash are issued, by way of what is known as *mining*.

The limited supply notion of Bitcoin Cash draws parallels to the limited supply of precious metals, such as gold, and the process by which new Bitcoin Cash are issued, called *mining*, draws its name from the physical process of mining for minerals.

That, however, is where the parallels stop, as there is nothing physical about bitcoin and new bitcoin are not dug out of the ground, but rather are generated by computer software running on computers dispersed around the world.

Anyone can run the Bitcoin Cash mining software, known as a *client*, but mining is so computationally resource intensive that not everyone can profitably run the software. The reason for this is because the software requires a large amount of computational power to produce Bitcoin Cash economically, and average desktop computers are not economically efficient enough to perform the calculations required.

The term *client* is a misnomer when it comes to bitcoin, because the Bitcoin Cash network does not follow traditional client-server architecture, but rather each client bares equal responsibility for keeping the network active, in a peer-to-peer architecture. To this extent, an instance of the mining software is better referred to as a *mining node*. Indeed, because even wallets may be referred to as clients on the Bitcoin Cash network, and where wallets do no mining tasks, mining nodes are often called *full mining nodes* to clarify what it is they do.

What is Bitcoin Cash Mining?

Bitcoin Cash mining is a process by which three primary things happen:

1. New Bitcoin Cash transactions are placed on the distributed open ledger that effectively tracks which Bitcoin Cash addresses hold which amount of Bitcoin Cash;

2. New Bitcoin Cash are issued to one miner each 10 minutes of the day, on average, and while there are still bitcoin cash to create, as a reward for maintaining the network;

3. The Bitcoin Cash network is secured against double spending, and other attack vectors on the network, by virtue of running the software that performs the mining process.

There is quite a bit happening behind the scenes to achieve those three primary aims of full mining nodes, but in a nutshell that is the process performed by those full mining nodes.

Central to the design of Bitcoin

Mining is central to the design of bitcoin, and we covered Satoshi Nakamoto's invention of creating a distributed and open ledger maintained by mining nodes performing a proof-of-work in the chapter The Great Scaling Debate. Mining is central to bitcoin because, quite obviously, for Bitcoin Cash to be an effective network over which value can be exchanged by people holding Bitcoin Cash, a ledger of which wallet holds which amount of Bitcoin Cash must be maintained.

In an early conversation on the metzdowd cryptography mailing list, Hal Finney calls people running the bitcoin software *node operators* and says

> [if] bitcoin system turns out to be socially useful
> and valuable, so that node operators feel that they
> are making a beneficial contribution to the world by
> their efforts (similar to the various "@Home" compute
> projects where people volunteer their compute
> resources for good causes) [then …] simple altruism
> can suffice to keep the network running properly.[110]

Running the bitcoin software is not, however, purely altruistic. Miners are incentivised to run the software by receiving new bitcoin and fees in bitcoin in exchange for the electricity they expend in running the software.

Miners show a Proof-of-work

What has been recognised as a work of genius, Satoshi Nakamoto's invention of bitcoin requires many things to happen at once so that only one linear timeline of transactions ultimately flow into a ledger.

The biggest problem solved by Nakamoto's invention of bitcoin is the *double spend problem*, which is characterised by the inherent problem of digital assets that they are easily copied and disseminated. If you have a photo stored digitally, say as a .jpg file, it is trivially easy for you to copy that file and send it to all your friends. When it comes to a digital network of money, what is needed is what is seemingly impossible, for it ***not*** to be possible for someone to copy the digital money they have and spend it somewhere twice, three times, or time and time again. This is known as the double spend problem.

---

[110] Hal Finney's thoughts on bitcoin, www.metzdowd.com, https://www.metzdowd.com/pipermail/cryptography/2008-November/014848.html, Accessed at Monday, 27 January 2020

To overcome this problem, Nakamoto implements a multi-pronged strategy within bitcoin. The first is to acknowledge that there is such a thing as double-spending; the second is to make it such that it is unprofitable for anyone to try and spend their bitcoin twice. The strategy adopted is known as Nakamoto Consensus using a *proof-of-work* and is characterised by making it both difficult and unprofitable to defraud the network.

Bitcoin relies on a game that is effectively played by mining nodes. Each *honest* mining node finds it more profitable to remain honest and for it to be fiscally rewarding for being honest. This way the network collectively attracts more honest nodes than dishonest nodes, effectively securing the network against double spending. The longer they stay honest, the more bitcoin cash miners can earn from newly minted bitcoin and in mining fees.

Electricity and time expended to prove work

New Bitcoin Cash is issued to a miner who effectively wins a digital lottery in competition with all other miners trying to win that same lottery. The difficulty of the lottery is increased by the mining software itself such that the more mining power that joins the lottery, the harder it is to win that lottery. It costs money to win the lottery because the computational difficulty requires electricity to run the computers. Suffice to say if the majority (over 50%) of the computational resources are playing the game honestly, then the Bitcoin Cash network is secure from double spending, because those with more than 50% of the computational power effectively form a cartel that keeps a valid ledger, rejecting double spends from malicious actors. The more nodes on the network of sufficient computational power and that are honest, the harder (and more expensive electricity-wise) it is for a malicious miner to wage an attack. A malicious actor must gauge whether they will make more money waging a malicious attack then they will spend on electricity doing so.

Quite obviously, if someone had the capacity and inclination to defraud the network, then they would and could create invalid blocks as fast as they could such that only their dishonest blocks choked up the blockchain such that the whole blockchain becomes invalid and useless.

Bitcoin overcomes this problem by effectively throttling the creation of blocks such that only one block of transactions is accepted by the network every 10 minutes on average, and by having an effective lottery over which miner gets to have mined the next block. Miners must expend electricity and processing power for each 10 minutes in order to be in the lottery and a special algorithm in the software basically proves that they have done both if they win the lottery.

The effect of throttling the network effectively creates a race against time itself for each mining node. A mining node can only win the lottery by producing the solution to a relatively simple problem but that which is extremely computationally expensive to process. Because the problem requires significant computational resource to solve, there is a tangible cost by way of electricity consumed by the computers trying to solve the problem. This cost also weighs against dishonest players because if they lose the lottery, with another but honest miner winning the lottery, then the dishonest player loses all of their electricity cost because they are not awarded new Bitcoin Cash, mining fees for transactions and any malicious transactions they have created.

By accepting a strategy whereby each node accepts blocks of transactions that show a proof-of-work, miners only fall prey to a dishonest miner in their mist if that dishonest miner has enough computing power to keep winning the lottery over and over again, not allowing honest blocks of transactions onto the ledger.

What is an Honest Miner?

It is trivially easy to be an honest miner, because the most widely used Bitcoin Cash mining client software is designed to check against double-spending within the Bitcoin Cash network. All other mining clients accept that block of transactions if the miner wins the proof-of-work lottery, while maintaining their own copy of the distributed ledger.

So, an honest miner is merely full mining node software that protects the network against double spending of Bitcoin Cash by running honest software and doing their proof-of-work.

Economically, if it became apparent that dishonest nodes were in charge of the network, then the value of Bitcoin Cash relative to other currencies would collapse to $0, which is not in the interest of miners. In this way also, miners are incentivised to stay honest, lest all of their earned Bitcoin Cash become worthless.

Mining is now highly specialised

Bitcoin is over 10 years old, and over that time both the software and hardware used to mine bitcoin has changed. Where at first release of bitcoin in 2009 it was profitable to mine bitcoin on a home computer, later versions of the software made it such that it was more profitable to mine bitcoin with first GPUs (Graphical Processing Unit hardware) and then with ASIC (Application Specific Integrated Circuits). ASICs are computer hardware designed specifically for a limited purpose and do that job very efficiently. ASIC bitcoin mining hardware is designed to specifically to mine bitcoin and is far more efficient at doing so than a personal computer.

In this manner bitcoin mining has become highly specialised and out of reach of the common person. While it is possible to buy ASIC miners and run them at home, because the hardware is outdated quite rapidly by newer models, without the economies of scale it is largely unprofitable to run bitcoin mining software at home, unless of course you have free electricity.

Mining Pools

Smaller mining node operators can pool together in what is known as a *mining pool* and with their combined computational power have a reasonable chance of winning the proof-of-work lottery and earning an income from bitcoin mining.

Mining Farms

Prophetically Nakamoto wrote on the bitcointalk.org forum in May, 2010:

If the network becomes very large, like over 100,000 nodes, [...] most users should start running client-only software [such as wallets] and only the specialist server farms keep running full network nodes ...[111]

Specialist mining farms are now a reality and the vast majority of computer processing power dedicated to mining bitcoin (including Bitcoin Cash) comes from mining farms. They are called *farms* because rather than one giant computer doing all the work, a mining farm has veritable herd of computers (ASIC miners) dedicated to mining bitcoin.

Checking on the Mining Health of Bitcoin Cash

Because much of the information about the public ledger of bitcoin cash is public information, including the mining difficulty, websites have been established that allows the average person to gauge the relative health of bitcoin mining. Such things that determine the health include the number of full mining nodes that are processing bitcoin cash transactions, which mining pools are

---

[111] Nakamoto predicts mining farms, www.bitcointalk.org, https://bitcointalk.org/index.php?topic=125.msg1149#msg1149, Accessed at Monday, 27 January 2020

winning the proof-of-work lottery and the relative profitability of mining bitcoin cash over bitcoin core.

One such website is https://cash.coin.dance/

The number of full mining nodes mining bitcoin cash can be found at https://cash.coin.dance/nodes. Which mining pools, if known, have won the periodic proof-of-work lottery can be found at https://cash.coin.dance/blocks. The relative profitability of mining bitcoin cash can also be found at https://cash.coin.dance/blocks and at https://bitinfocharts.com/comparison/bitcoin%20cash-mining_profitability.html

Similar Bitcoin Cash health charts can be found at https://charts.bitcoin.com/bch/

Energy spent mining Bitcoin

A vast amount of electricity is currently consumed by proof-of-work mining operations over bitcoin cash and bitcoin core. While ASIC miners are efficient at performing the calculations for proof-of-work they none the less consume a lot of electricity in order to process as many iterations of the required work per second. The amount of electricity consumed per annum is more than many countries. The central problem is that to stay ahead in the proof-of-work calculation game miners must purchase ever faster ASIC hardware devices and more of them.

One pundit calculated that in August 2018 the Bitcoin Cash mining network consumed in the vicinity of 4.3 billion kWh (kilowatt hours) of electricity per year; or more than the country of Moldova [112].

---

[112] Tim Swanson's blog and Twitter entries calculating the electricity usage of various cryptocurrencies, https://www.ofnumbers.com/2018/08/26/how-much-electricity-is-consumed-by-bitcoin-bitcoin-cash-ethereum-litecoin-and-

By any standards this is an outrageous amount of electricity, and the problem was foreseen in the very month that bitcoin was released in 2009. Hal Finney, probably the first person other than Satoshi Nakamoto to run the bitcoin node software wrote on the metzdowd.com mailing list in January 2009:

If POW [proof-of-work] tokens do become useful, and especially if they become money, machines will no longer sit idle. Users will expect their computers to be earning them money (assuming the reward is greater than the cost to operate) [113].

This almost immediately drew prophetic criticism, with a response:

Computers are already designed to consume much less electricity when idle than when running full tilt. This trend will continue and extend; some modern chips throttle down to zero MHz and virtually zero watts at idle, waking automatically at the next interrupt.

The last thing we need is to deploy a system designed to burn all available cycles, consuming electricity and generating carbon dioxide, all over the Internet, in order to produce small amounts of bitbux to get emails or spams through.

Can't we just convert actual money in a bank account into bitbux -- cheaply and without a carbon tax? Please? [114]

Hal Finney was open to the criticism with:

It's interesting to consider the ultimate technological resolution

monero/ , https://twitter.com/ofnumbers/status/1032837686963331072 , Accessed at Monday, 27 January 2020

[113] Hal Finney talking about proof-of-work, www.metzdowd.com, https://www.metzdowd.com/pipermail/cryptography/2009-January/015036.html, Accessed at Monday, 27 January 2020

[114] Early criticism of proof-of-work mining, www.metzdowd.com, https://www.metzdowd.com/pipermail/cryptography/2009-January/015042.html , Accessed at Monday, 27 January 2020

to this issue. Will a global-scale proof-of-work based system inherently consume substantial amounts of energy? [115]

This question has well and truly been answered and it remains a sizable problem for bitcoin that it consumes such vast amounts of electricity to stay alive as a transaction network. A valid and poignant argument against the *store of value* concept of bitcoin is that if all the mining nodes of bitcoin were shut down there would be no value in bitcoin. The vast amounts of electricity consumed by the bitcoin networks must continually be consumed for each bitcoin to have value. Contrast this to gold, which is mined out of the ground just once and requires no expense to maintain its value to people over time.

---

[115] Hal Finney, more on proof-of-work, www.metzddowd.com, https://www.metzdowd.com/pipermail/cryptography/2009-January/015056.html , Accessed at Monday, 27 January 2020

News Services

There are a number of online news services that will help you find information on Bitcoin Cash. The only one we list here is:

https://news.bitcoin.com/

A simple internet search for *cryptocurrency news* or *bitcoin cash news* returns many news websites, but we list the bitcoin.com website here because of its bias towards bitcoin cash news reporting.

The Bitcoin.com website capitalises, quite obviously, on dominantly holding the name Bitcoin in its domain name. The website itself is a treasure chest of information about Bitcoin Cash, including a news section which can be accessed by clicking on the [News] menu option at the top of the front page.

Although I did not witness it, it is clear that Bitcoin.com used to promote Bitcoin Core up until the creation of Bitcoin Cash. A myriad of YouTube videos produced by the chairman of bicoin.com, Roger Ver, makes it clear that Bitcoin.com will allocate its resources into the promotion and adoption of Bitcoin Cash. So the news articles on this site naturally tend to favour Bitcoin Cash over other cryptocurrencies, and provide the latest news on Bitcoin Cash.

The news.bitcoin.com has article contributors from all over the world and you will find many useful articles on cryptocurrencies in general, including their impact on the world.

To the extent that news.bitcoin.com has a political bent, detracting from banks and fiat currencies in general, I find that the source adequately reflects the revolution that proponents of cryptocurrencies feel that they are fighting for. However, where the site digresses into politics actively criticizing the incarceration of Russel Ulbricht (of Silk Road infamy), I feel that the site detracts from sound an objective reporting. I am also unsure as to whether promoting stories of the alleged unfairness of Mr Ulbricht's sentence has any direct relevance to a cause for cryptocurrencies, but would rather strengthen the resolve of those within government that wish to see the end of cryptocurrencies. At the very least, the news on this site is like that of any other news site and should be read with whatever critical position or objectivity that you apply to other news sources.

Problems facing Bitcoin Cash

Like any currency Bitcoin Cash has its fair share of problems. Technically the currency may be sound, but there are a range of sociological problems that must be addressed to further the cause of Bitcoin Cash.

Recognition in the marketplace

Bitcoin used to be the de facto brand name of only one cryptocurrency. Now the name bitcoin is used for multiple cryptocurrencies. The marketing challenge faced by Bitcoin Cash is that people who are first learning about cryptocurrencies are faced with a brand recognition problem. Which cryptocurrency should they use and trust?

The bitcoincash.org website tries to disambiguate with the following:

```
"Bitcoin Cash is usually represented by the
BCH ticker symbol and is considered by its
supporters to be the legitimate continuation of
the Bitcoin project as peer-to-peer digital
cash." 116
```

This statement is bold and direct and it seems that all Bitcoin Cash proponents can do is replay the message over and over to disambiguate from cryptocurrencies such as Bitcoin Core.

---

[116] Disambiguating Bitcoin Cash from Bitcoin Core on the bitcoincash.org website, https://www.bitcoincash.org/faq.html, Accessed at Monday, 27 January 2020

Mixed Marketing Message

The bitcoin.com website seems to act as a significant marketing promotional mouthpiece for Bitcoin Cash cryptocurrency. Their site has statements such as:

```
"Today, Bitcoin Cash (BCH) can meet the demands
of a global currency, which is why we support it
here at Bitcoin.com." [117]
```

The central problem here seems to be that for a currency to be *global* and widely accepted across the world, it needs to have support of billions of people. The vast majority of this large targeted market would be law abiding citizens frowning on criminal activity. How is that a problem? Well, bitcoin.com (in 2020) supports causes which seem to promote extremes of criminal and violent behaviour. This is an incompatible marketing message which will make it very difficult, in this author's eyes, for Bitcoin Cash to ever be a globally accepted currency as law enforcement personnel will most likely and eventually target any entity that supports the extremes of criminality and violence.

For example, visiting freedom.bitcoin.com on the bitcoin.com website we find that bitcoin.com claims to "proudly support" the following causes:

1. Development of 3D printed guns. The last I have heard 3D printed can be used to kill people or used to smuggle a gun onto an airplane to commit an act of terrorism. It is hard to imagine what else a 3D printed plastic gun is for exactly. Freedom.bitcoin.com states "we stand up for freedom and liberty", but what kind of society supports 3D printed plastic guns? On the 24th of January 2020 Frankly Media shared a global news story that 20 states of the United States of America, a federation priding itself on 'freedom

---

[117] Bitcoin.com spruiking Bitcoin Cash, https://www.bitcoin.com/get-started/what-is-bitcoin/, Accessed at Monday, 27 January 2020

and liberty', filed suit against a federal regulation that could allow the blueprints of 3D printed plastic guns to be posted to the internet [118]. Quite obviously there are many people concerned about the potential use of 3D printed guns for violent crime. This *cause* of bitcoin.com seems out of touch with a goal of any peaceful endeavour of making bitcoin cash a global currency if bitcoin.com chooses to be a mouthpiece for bitcoin cash; and it is hard to see the common man or woman on the street being in support of this.

2. Freeing Ross Ulbricht (of Silk Road infamy) from prison. Ross Ulbricht was sentenced to 2 life sentences plus 40 years in the United States of America for starting and running a darknet website called Silk Road. The Silk Road website allowed a vast array of criminal merchandise to be sold and dispersed across the globe and use of some of the drugs sold over the network resulted in the deaths of the drug users who bought them. Bitcoin.com seemingly supports selling illegal drugs over the internet and considers Ulbricht's crimes victimless. At least the complaint on freedom.bitcoin.com is that "no victim was named at trial".

These *causes* of bitcoin.com seem incompatible with supporting the launch a widely accepted currency. Is it that bitcoin.com wants Bitcoin Cash to be used for crime? The news outlet of bitcoin.com regularly publishes stories on the use of the darknet, where the darknet is an area of the internet that supports criminal sites such as the former Silk Road, and promotion of privacy technology for bitcoin cash [119]. The problem with promoting technology that would make bitcoin cash completely private, or untraceable by

---

[118] Frankly Media reports on 20 U.S. states suing over federal regulation that might allow the publishing of blueprints for 3D printed guns on the internet, http://www.wboc.com/story/41607120/coalition-of-states-sue-over-rules-governing-3dprinted-guns , Accessed at Monday, 27 January 2020

[119] Search news.bitcoin.com for *dark* (https://news.bitcoin.com/?s=dark) for stories on the darknet; some actually seeming to promote the darknet.

authorities, is that cryptocurrency exchanges around the world have dropped support for cryptocurrencies, such as Monero, that have anonymous and largely untraceable transactions [120]. It seems that this would be a huge impediment to bitcoin cash being adopted as a global currency if nobody can buy Bitcoin Cash at an exchange. Bitcoin.com's marketing approach seems incompatible with a stated goal of supporting bitcoin cash to become a global currency. In as much as the values of a news outlet is reflected in the stories it publishes, this author has seen no article published on news.bitcoin.com that condemns the illicit use of cryptocurrency to commit crime on the darknet.

Usability

As someone who has worked with computer systems most of my life, this author agrees with critics who complain that bitcoin has a usability problem. Let us investigate some of those problems here:

Too easy to lose

If you have a bitcoin wallet on your smartphone and have not backed up the mnemonic to reclaim the wallet if your phone is lost or stolen, then you have most likely lost all your bitcoin associated with that wallet. It is that easy. There is nobody to telephone and ask for help. You are completely responsible for the funds against your wallet. Not such a bad thing for small amounts of currency, but potentially devastating where large amounts of cryptocurrency are involved.

Even if you use a hardware wallet to store larger amounts of bitcoin away from your computer or personal computer, you have the problem of not having your hardware wallet lost or stolen.

---

[120] Search news.bitcoin.com for privacy (https://news.bitcoin.com/?s=privacy) for stories about moves to make bitcoin cash transactions private, and moves to delist privacy cryptocurrencies from exchanges around the world.

Even if you do backup your wallets' mnemonic, you have the responsibility of not loosing that.

These are genuine concerns about using bitcoin.

A lot to learn

Bitcoin is deceptively easy to use if you simply download a bitcoin wallet and start sending and receiving bitcoin. But there is much to learn which could otherwise leave unwary person losing all their bitcoin.

For instance, if someone downloads a wallet and puts a large amount of bitcoin against that wallet. That much is easy enough. But what if they remove the application from their smartphone or computer without first having backed up the mnemonic to reclaim the wallet? There bitcoin is gone!

It is simple things like this which are very different from working with traditional banks and bank accounts, and which require quite a bit of upfront learning. If you accidentally remove your banking app from your smartphone, chances are that your bank will help you to set things up again. You will not have lost your money.

Even getting bitcoin to a wallet is a challenge unless you are being paid for some good or service. To purchase bitcoin from an exchange in many countries you need to not only find an exchange that you trust, but then supply the exchange provider with identification. You then need to learn a thing or two about exchange rates, and exchange fees, storing your bitcoin on the exchange and moving it to your wallet. All these learning touchpoints are friction to bitcoin cash becoming a globally used currency.

Cryptocurrencies have an awkward community

Not specific to bitcoin cash, but the cryptocurrency space in general, there is an awkward and off-putting atmosphere about cryptocurrencies. Beside the sigma that cryptocurrencies are the purview of software geeks, the main discussion forums for cryptocurrencies are social networks such as Reddit.com and Twitter.com where offensive venom words like *troll* are thrown around readily at users of the platform.

As a humorous example, I just went to the Reddit forum most commonly used for bitcoin cash proponents, https://www.reddit.com/r/btc/, and did a search for 'troll'. Sure enough, a posting headed *"Oh look, another troll"* was returned straight away. Is this the maturity of those seeking to support a global currency? One wonders.

Government Regulation

One of the biggest problems facing Bitcoin Cash going forward is conceivably government regulation of cryptocurrencies.

While still not a sizable thread to sovereign currencies, some governments around the world have banned the use of cryptocurrencies at any rate.

While perhaps not able to entirely stamp out cryptocurrencies, governments can make it very difficult for people to use cryptocurrencies in day to day commerce, and basically make it unattractive enough that people just give up on their use in some countries.

Investing (?) in Bitcoin Cash

In 2018 it would have seemed ludicrous to speak of *investing* in Bitcoin or any cryptocurrency. Over the course of 2018, the market price of nearly every cryptocurrency in U.S. dollars declined anything from 60% to 95% relative to the same time in 2017. Any reasonable person would say that that is not an investment but a catastrophe.

2018 was a pivotal year for cryptocurrencies, because it is was the first year that not only did Bitcoin Core go down in price but the collective market capitalisation of alternate cryptocurrencies (alt coins) also declined. It was the year that many predicted that many cryptocurrencies will '*go to zero*' (i.e. have their exchange price go to $0) and never recover, effectively shaking out the market. I started writing this book in 2018 and personally I found it mindless that there were over 1000 cryptocurrencies, and so it was interesting to watch the shakeout happen.

While markets did recover in 2019, many of the thousands of cryptocurrencies did effectively *go to zero* and were delisted from exchange websites. What is interesting now is that people have not tired of trying to make money out of cryptocurrencies with there being over 5000 cryptocurrencies in existence in early 2020.

Of course, people are trying to replicate the phenomenal rise in the exchange price of Bitcoin Core, which rose from mere cents in 2010 to a high of U.S. $20,000 in 2017, making some people a fortune along the way. The subsequent crash of Bitcoin Core to U.S. $3000 in 2018 was a wakeup call of the risk in *investing* in cryptocurrencies.

Hal Finney prophetically predicted mere days after Bitcoin Core was released to the world that bitcoin may be worth a substantial amount per bitcoin in the future, writing on metzdowd.com mailing list:

As an amusing thought experiment, imagine that Bitcoin is successful and becomes the dominant payment system in use throughout the world. Then the total value of the currency should be equal to the total value of all the wealth in the world. Current estimates of total worldwide household wealth that I have found range from $100 trillion to $300 trillion. With 20 million coins, that gives each coin a value of about $10 million. So the possibility of generating coins today with a few cents of compute time may be quite a good bet, with a payoff of something like 100 million to 1! Even if the odds of Bitcoin succeeding to this degree are slim, are they really 100 million to one against? Something to think about... Hal [121]

But this chapter is about investing in Bitcoin Cash. Is this something you should do? What are the risks? When is a good time to buy? These are some of the questions that you should ask yourself.

What type of investment is a cryptocurrency?

An investment in a cryptocurrency is effectively purchasing an asset that you would hope to sell to some other person at a higher price than what you paid for it. To my knowledge there is no cryptocurrency that pays any form of interest or dividend, and so the only hope of making money from an 'investment' into a cryptocurrency is by selling it for more than you purchased it. That is it.

Historically, for holders of Bitcoin Core, this strategy has gone very well for some people who purchased Bitcoin at a $1 per Bitcoin and where the price is now over $6000 in 2020. This has made some people millionaires and billionaires. It seems,

---

[121] Hal Finney predicts a hefty price per bitcoin in the future, www.metzdowd.com, https://www.mail-archive.com/cryptography@metzdowd.com/msg10152.html, Accessed at Monday, 27 January 2020

however, that those days are well and truly behind us and that we will never again see percent gains in the thousands, at least for any form of Bitcoin. My personal feeling is that we will be lucky to see gains in the double digits ever again.

Bitcoin has been described as an unintentional Ponzi scheme, where holders of Bitcoin actively promote bitcoin to new purchasers and where the rewards end up with early investors; with late comers losing out with nobody to sell their stake to. If you were unlucky enough to have purchased Bitcoin Cash at $4000 in 2017, or Bitcoin Core for $19000, you would be forgiven for thinking that indeed the cryptocurrency bubble of 2017 was a reflection of some type of Ponzi scheme. It seems that Bitcoin is seen as an unintentional Ponzi scheme because the empirical evidence left by the original people responsible for the creation of Bitcoin saw it that they were genuinely creating a new form of currency, and all speculative purchasing of Bitcoin since then is incidental. This point of view holds a half-truth, however, because Bitcoin was always designed with limited supply in mind, with an intention for the value of a held Bitcoin to appreciate over time and with strengthening demand.

Some cryptocurrencies have been seen as intentional 'pump and dump' schemes, leaving later 'investors' holding the bag and having lost their investment.

In this chapter we explore the many ways to evaluate whether Bitcoin Cash is worth purchasing and how to evaluate the risk of purchasing a cryptocurrency.

Take away – Cryptocurrencies should not be looked upon as any investment that you would not normally associate with the purchasing of a currency (e.g. the Japanese yen), and where there is extreme risk in investing in a cryptocurrency. Currencies such as Bitcoin Cash may increase in price over time given the decreasing supply of Bitcoin Cash in the future, but this will only be predicated by a stable and/or increased demand. Conversely, if Bitcoin Cash never realises the dream and intention of widespread adoption, you should expect that the price of Bitcoin Cash will decrease and represent no investment at all.

What are the risks in investing in Bitcoin Cash?

With any effective asset over which there is no guarantee of a future sale price higher than the initial purchase price, there exists significant risk in purchasing that asset.

It is clear that the intention of the self appointed Bitcoin Cash developers and promoters is for Bitcoin Cash to become widely adopted over time, driving demand and price increase, but intention is no guarantee of success.

For a currency to be successful and widely adopted, naturally we would expect that the price at least remain stable and not decline or fluctuate wildly in price. The only credit to Bitcoin Cash's name at the time of writing is that after a year and a half of Bitcoin Cash trading on exchanges around the world, the price is not lower than the initial listed price on exchanges. Only time will tell whether Bitcoin Cash will hold value.

Price fluctuations are by no means the only risk in investing your money in purchasing Bitcoin Cash. You should also consider the risk of losing your private keys and/or wallet, or having them stolen, and losing all of your investment. If you hold your Bitcoin Cash within an online wallet on a cryptocurrency exchange, you run the risk of that exchange being hacked and your Bitcoin Cash stolen.

So there is great responsibility in holding a cryptocurrency such as Bitcoin Cash, as you effectively become your own investment advisor (when gauging wether to purchase on price) and your own bank when considering the responsibility you hold for managing the risk over the private keys providing access to your Bitcoin Cash.

When is a good time to buy Bitcoin Cash?

Unless you are an experienced and successful day trader or an expectant long term investor in Bitcoin Cash, there is no good time to buy Bitcoin Cash in my view. In the short history of Bitcoin Cash, the price has ebbed and flowed and the price seems just as likely to go down as up. Sophisticated day traders may make money, but many will do no better than gambling. The same is true for long term investors. The long term gamble is that Bitcoin Cash will be widely adopted over time and given the limited supply of Bitcoin Cash the price will increase relative to other asset classes.

The Bitcoin Cash Conundrum

The conundrum for Bitcoin Cash is that if it becomes extremely popular as a currency and widely adopted across the world, to the detriment of all fiat currencies across the world, then investing in Bitcoin Cash becomes a misnomer, as what would you trade Bitcoin Cash for? Another currency that is worthless?

The history of investing in cryptocurrencies

The entire cryptocurrency market is less than 12 years old, and so there is precious little data from which to form a long term perspective over historical price movements of cryptocurrencies.

A world wide social experiment is being held before our eyes. When Satoshi Nakamoto introduced Bitcoin to the world, Nakamoto deliberately styled Bitcoin after the gold standard, limiting the ultimate supply of Bitcoin.

Even though the current inflation rate of Bitcoin is around 4%, the currency has been acting in a deflationary way, and increasing in price year on year and over time. Whether this historical trend will continue into the future is yet to be seen.

Inflation as a Factor

Forked cryptocurrencies create inflation. When Bitcoin Cash was created as a currency that split off from Bitcoin Core, the exchange price of Bitcoin Core collapsed considerably. What guarantees are there in the future that nobody will fork off another cryptocurrency from Bitcoin Cash and cause the Bitcoin Cash exchange price to collapse?

Fundamentals to watch

In this section we investigate fundamental statistical data to be aware of and to watch over time in order to gauge the level of risk that exists over the Bitcoin Cash network and currency.

Number of active addresses

The number of active addresses may provide an insight into the total number of people who own Bitcoin Cash. For any investor hoping for a price increase in Bitcoin Cash, a certain metric reflecting whether or not demand for Bitcoin Cash is rising or falling is the number of active addresses. The more active addresses, the better chance that the price of Bitcoin Cash will be stable over time, as fewer players have a chance to influence the exchange price. The argument is that increased demand and use of Bitcoin Cash is likely to increase the purchasing power of the currency.

You can find a chart of the active addresses for Bitcoin Cash at bitinfocharts.com:

https://bitinfocharts.com/comparison/activeaddresses-bch.html

Take away - You should note that the number of active addresses for Bitcoin Cash fell steadily over the year 2018. This was not a good sign for Bitcoin Cash.

Transactions per second

A sure gauge of whether Bitcoin Cash is being readily adopted and used throughout the world is to view the number of transactions taking place on the network and per second of the day.

The number of transactions per day on the Bitcoin Cash network can be seen at bitinfocharts.com:

https://bitinfocharts.com/comparison/transactions-bch.html

Take away - The number or transactions per day on the Bitcoin Cash network increased by about 100% over the year of 2018, but remained static for practically all of 2019. You must factor into whether the 2018 increase in transactions represents increased adoption or merely represents more Bitcoin Cash miners maintaining the network and being issued block rewards from the mining pool to which they belong (See the chapter on Bitcoin Mining for more information), when making any decision over this data.

Google Trends

You would naturally expect that the number of people searching for information about Bitcoin Cash on Google (www.google.com) would reflect the relative public interest in the currency. Indeed, the number of searches on Bitcoin Cash on Google has, to some degree, been reflected in the price of Bitcoin Cash.

Google provides an online statistical charging tool called Google Trends, and with which you can produce a statistical graph on the number of searches on a term made through Google's search facilities. This can be found at:
https://trends.google.com

Simply type in "Bitcoin Cash" and select "Worldwide" to view a historical graph of the number of searches on the term, "Bitcoin Cash".

An interesting feature of the Google Trends facility is a world map which shows the relative intensity of searches for a given term from within the various countries of the world. For instance, it may be gauged that the relatively high search rate for Bitcoin Cash from within Venezuela may reflect the comparative instability of Venezuela's fiat currency and where people are looking to cryptocurrencies as an alternative to that fiat currency. The same could not be said for Australia, however, and where a high search rate on Bitcoin Cash may reflect the relatively high technical proficiency of Australians. Any analysis of Google Trends in this regard must be subjective, but the statistical data is helpful in providing insight into the interest in Bitcoin Cash throughout the world.

Take away - You should note that the number of searches on the term, "Bitcoin Cash", declined over the year 2018, and remained relatively static over 2019.

Mining Difficulty

The mining difficulty for Bitcoin Cash, or the amount of effort required by miners to win the proof-of-work lottery for Bitcoin Cash, may provide some indication as to what miners are willing to sell newly minted bitcoin cash for. A higher mining difficulty may equate to higher electricity costs that need covering, however there is no proven correlation between mining difficulty and the price of bitcoin. The mining difficulty of Bitcoin Cash can be found at:

https://bitinfocharts.com/comparison/bitcoin%20cash-difficulty.html

Synopsis

This book provides no advice on investing in cryptocurrencies or Bitcoin Cash. The only thing this author will point out is that the endeavour is extremely risky and speculative.

About the author

Victor Morgante holds a degree in Information Technology (Distinction) from the Queensland University of Technology, Australia, and has spent over 25 years in the information technology arena. Mr Morgante's early IT career was spent working with telecommunications companies and he now works almost exclusively with conceptual modelling and database design. Victor's passion, however, is marketing and developing products, valuing people over technology.

While technical, Victor is also highly sceptical of new technologies. Victor's outlook is conservative, and that is why he wrote this book, to bring balance to the hype surrounding cryptocurrencies.

www.ingramcontent.com/pod-product-compliance
Lightning Source LLC
Chambersburg PA
CBHW030625220526
45463CB00004B/1422